Project Management Institute

MW01122498

WHAT ENABLES PROJECT SUCCESS: LESSONS FROM AID RELIEF PROJECTS

Paul Steinfort, PhD, PMP, BE (Hons)
and
Derek H. T. Walker, PhD, MSc,
Grad Dip (Mgt Sys)

Library of Congress Cataloging-in-Publication Data

Steinfort, Paul.
  What enables project success : lessons from aid relief projects / Paul Steinfort and Derek
H.T. Walker.
      p. cm.
  Includes bibliographical references.
  ISBN 978-1-935589-27-3 (alk. paper)
  1. Project management. 2. International relief. I. Walker, Derek H. T. II. Title.
  HD69.P75S739 2011
  658.4'04--dc22

                                          2011013119

ISBN: 978-1-935589-27-3

Published by: Project Management Institute, Inc.
                       14 Campus Boulevard
                       Newtown Square, Pennsylvania 19073-3299 USA
                       Phone: +610-356-4600
                       Fax: +610-356-4647
                       Email: customercare@pmi.org
                       Internet: www.PMI.org

PMI Publications welcomes corrections and comments on its books. Please feel free to
send comments on typographical, formatting, or other errors. Simply make a copy of the
relevant page of the book, mark the error, and send it to: Book Editor, PMI Publications,
14 Campus Boulevard, Newtown Square, PA 19073-3299 USA.

To inquire about discounts for resale or educational purposes, please contact the PMI Book
Service Center.
                       PMI Book Service Center
                       P.O. Box 932683, Atlanta, GA 31193-2683 USA
                       Phone: 1-866-276-4764 (within the U.S. or Canada)
                       or +1-770-280-4129 (globally)
                       Fax: +1-770-280-4113
                       Email: book.orders@pmi.org

10 9 8 7 6 5 4 3 2 1

Contents

Acknowledgments

We would like to thank and acknowledge the Project Management Institute for generously funding part of our research. We would also like to thank Paul's community of practice—his group of colleagues, friends, family, and clients, current and past, who through the many thousands of emails over these past three years have generously donated their time, energy, and wisdom in responding to Paul's reflections, interpretations, ideas, data, and speculations.

We would especially like to thank Noela Steinfort.

Also, we thank and acknowledge Dr. Beverley Lloyd-Walker for her comments, support, and tolerance of Derek's being at times seemingly married to his laptop for hours upon end.

We both have many colleagues at our respective workplaces who acted as occasional sounding boards. RMIT University was instrumental in providing Paul with a PhD research scholarship to undertake his research and access to the RMIT library and other facilities at the School of Property, Construction, and Project Management.

1

Introduction

1.1 Chapter Introduction

Why do we "do" projects? What is their purpose? Is there something different or special about aid relief projects that we can learn from? Can traditional project management approaches offer such projects something specific? These are valid and interesting questions for the project management discipline to address. Perhaps one more critical question to answer is, what are the antecedents of project and project management success?

One reason why we do projects is that they are vehicles for delivering a specifically defined value or benefit. Project management is, as defined by the Project Management Institute (PMI), "the application of knowledge, skills, tools, and techniques in order to meet or exceed stakeholder requirements from a project," and a project is defined as "a temporary endeavor undertaken to create a unique product or service" (PMI, 2004, p. 368). This suggests that project work is special, targeted to a specific need, and has a defined life cycle from initiation to closure. We do projects to fulfill a need and to provide a defined benefit. This raises the question of whose need is being fulfilled. Much project management front-end work involves identifying the "who" and "what" in terms of the need to be met. The more traditional project management world practitioners tend to think that the answers to these two questions are obvious, but they are not. In fact, the aid project world spends a lot more time and effort on these front-end issues of defining the beneficiaries and the nature of the benefit to be realized than the more traditional project management world does.

When we began the research leading to this book, we assumed that the aid project management world would benefit from traditional project management insights, tools, and techniques because we could see that there was little application of these artifacts in aid projects. We felt that this might explain the apparent chaos and difficulties observed by some of our colleagues in their anecdotes of the lived reality of their aid project world. We later discovered that their world appeared to address the front end of projects better than the traditional project management world did, which came as a surprise to us. When we reconsidered what the antecedents to project management and project success might be, in light of how the aid project management world appears to operate, we discovered that we had some important lessons to learn from the aid world. This book traces that journey of discovery.

This chapter is structured as follows. The first section will discuss in more detail the purpose of projects in terms of value and benefits. This will be followed by an explanation of the book's context and structure and, finally, by a chapter summary.

1.2 The Purpose of Projects

Projects can be seen as generators of value and learning (Winter, Andersen, Elvin, & Levene, 2006). *A Guide to the Project Management Body of Knowledge (PMBOK® Guide)* describes a project as creating a unique product, service, or result (PMI, 2008a). The *PMBOK Guide®* also describes a project as "a temporary endeavor undertaken to create a unique product or service" (p. 5). Projects are temporary in that they have a start and defined endpoint when the output is delivered. However, there is some confusion relating to the benefits that are delivered by projects, programs, and portfolios of programs or projects. The confusion arises out of the distinction between outputs and outcomes—though, as Nogeste argues, these can be linked in a way that better clarifies the real purpose that led to the temporary endeavor (Nogeste & Walker, 2005). She used a methodology based upon PRINCE2 (Bentley, 1997) to demonstrate how this methodology could be used through her developed templates to link outputs with outcomes (Nogeste, 2006).

There remains the problem of demonstrating how project management success can lead to project success (de Wit, 1988; Cooke-Davies, 2002). The process of managing a project can be successful, yet the output may not lead to the project outcome being seen as successful. In the project management aid world a good example of this is where reconstruction after a catastrophe can result in sound project management practices by a highly sophisticated construction contractor leading to reconstruction of new houses for a village project. However, if the supporting infrastructure needed for these to function (i.e., "hard" services such as transportation links, water, power, etc., and "soft" services such as restoring the morale and dignity of the community) is not delivered in an entrained sequence when needed, then the houses will not be homes and the village will be a population center and not a vibrant and functioning community. The link between output and outcome may be ignored or misunderstood.

The ideal way of viewing this situation may be that a series of projects should produce a series of outputs which, when melded together synergistically, produce the desired outcome. The outcome is the "real" benefit, whereas the "real" value is the manner in which these outputs are combined into an outcome, which direct project stakeholders recognize as having been delivered. The International Monetary Fund (IMF) clarifies the distinction as follows: "In performance assessment in government, outputs are defined as the goods or services produced by government agencies (e.g., teaching hours delivered, welfare benefits assessed and paid); outcomes are defined as the impacts on social, economic, or other indicators arising from the delivery of outputs (e.g., student learning, social equity) (IMF, 2007).

Customer value is the value that the purchaser perceives from a transaction, and it is therefore generated from an outcome of a project and its potential value to the end users. The outcome from a project needs to be realized in use—that is, in its application—so that its impact becomes apparent.

We talk a lot about benefits realization in project management (Remenyi & Sherwood-Smith, 1998; Bradley, 2006) and take this to mean the stated outputs, but as Nogeste (Nogeste & Walker, 2005; Nogeste, 2006) argues, outputs and outcomes are linked, but different, concepts. Projects deliver a number of benefits to a range of stakeholders. Those immediately concerned with project management, the project management team members, will derive the benefit of experience to potentially reflect on, and thereby gain value for future projects. These teams and organizations may gain benefits in fees and remuneration for delivering project outputs, and the entire project supply chain will share in such benefits. The paying customers, who have defined the scope, scale, and expectations of the project through a project brief, will gain benefits from the result of the project to use as an instrument to achieve benefit for themselves and the end users.

The concept of program management is becoming more pronounced in the traditional project management world (Pellegrinelli, 1997; Evaristo & van Fenema, 1999; KPMG, 2003; Office of Government Commerce, 2007; PMI, 2008b). In general, it is accepted that programs are the conceptual vehicles that group projects into a coherent and connected framework. The value and benefit derived from a post-tsunami reconstruction re-housing project output, when combined with the outputs from associated infrastructure projects (as a series of ancillary projects) and associated social projects (such as education, health, or cultural initiatives) may be realized as specific outcomes. One such outcome could be a resilient community that can overcome the trauma of a disaster and not only prepare itself for a return to normal life, but also for coping with any subsequent similar disasters. Benefits from separate projects can be synergized and coordinated through well-designed and managed programs of projects. A useful way of making expected outcomes explicit is to classify them in terms of being immediate, short term, and long term (Carroll & McKenna, 2001). As previously stated, Nogeste (Nogeste & Walker, 2005; Nogeste, 2006) uses a PRINCE 2 methodology (Bentley, 1997) as a way to link outputs with expected outcomes, so we have seen tools used by project managers being used to report on benefits realization in terms of outcomes.

As construction project managers, both authors tend (as would, we believe, most engineering and construction project managers) to view projects from an isolated point of view. That is, we have tendered for or negotiated to undertake projects that had been conceived and initiated by others "higher up" in the project management decision-making hierarchy. This mindset has dominated the project management discipline (Crawford, Morris, Thomas, & Winter, 2006) in more general terms and has caused concern more recently, because such a conception of a project tends to blind us from the real purpose of "our" projects—that they are instrumental for some beneficial change to specific project stakeholders.

The central objective of this book is to explore the antecedents of project management best practices, using aid projects as the contextual framework to more fully understand them. We started out on our journey expecting to be able to bring project management best practices to the aid world because one of us (Paul Steinfort) became intimately involved in two particular projects. The first was the reconstruction program in Aceh Indonesia after the devastating December 2004 tsunami, and the second was the response to the February 2009 bushfires disaster in our own state of Victoria, Australia, in which Paul's sister lost her home and almost her life. An unexpected discovery from our study was that the traditional project management world has much to learn from the aid recovery project world.

In this book, we hope to summarize the benefits in knowledge that we gained from this study (kindly and generously supported by PMI by means of a research grant) and to share that knowledge.

In particular, we aim to:

- Explain how the project management mindset is changing by enabling value derived from individual projects to enhance effective delivery of business or social program outcomes
- Offer a deeper understanding of the validity of seeing project objectives and outputs in a broader way than has been traditionally dominant in the project management literature, through our exposure to the vast aid relief and aid project literature
- Introduce pragmatic research methodological approaches to readers who may not have considered their usefulness before
- Explore the lived experience of project managers in extraordinarily challenging circumstances and indicate how they cope and what other project management professionals in more traditional contexts can learn from them
- Explain the nature and impact of the antecedents of project management best practices

1.3 The Context of This Book

This book was written by two authors coming initially from a traditional engineering and construction worldview of projects, though both of us have shifted our focus somewhat over our 40 years of practice toward the kinds of projects that are now common in business, government, and aid sectors. However, we both have open minds in terms of research approach possibilities.

Paul Steinfort heads a project management consultancy in Melbourne, Australia, (called PSA) and has undertaken projects amounting to several billions of dollars in areas including construction, IT, aid, business improvement, and strategic management. Derek Walker comes from a construction project management background initially in his native United Kingdom, but also in Canada and Australia. For the past 25 years, he has been based in academia, where he researches, edits an international project management journal, writes extensively, teaches, and supervises doctoral candidates. The main point here is that both authors have taken a journey, which has drawn them away from traditional project management practice and toward more non-traditional sectors. This has enabled them both to look at project management through a range of worldview lenses, so they are not committed to any paradigm, even though the natural tendency of most project managers is to view project management as being generally instrumental in nature.

The field research work that forms the basis for this book was undertaken in the context of aid relief and disaster recovery projects. Aid relief projects are very interesting from an exploratory project management point of view. First, they carry an acute sense of urgency—the outputs are often critical to project recipients sustaining their lives and livelihoods, and to the quality of life of affected communities. Second, the definition of what needs to be done, and the need, scope, and scale for recovery projects are also extremely challenging, because key stakeholders are often missing, dead, or traumatized to the extent that they cannot articulate their more profound needs. Third, the recovery aim may not involve a mere replication of what was lost, but rather a community's preparation to be resilient, to recover, and perhaps to improve their situation, and also to cope with any subsequent similar catastrophes.

Earthquakes, bushfires, tsunamis, and tropical storms are recurring threats that people in certain environments may face several times in their lives. Finally, these projects are particularly challenging in terms of stakeholder engagement and cultural sensitivity. These are but a few of the factors that make this type of project an interesting and valuable candidate for research, but they were the key factors in our minds when we decided to devote our time and energy to better understanding this important project management area; we believe that they constitute a sound justification for researching this sector of project management life.

Added to this, both authors bring considerable reflection on project management practice to this study. Much of what is presented in this book derives from Paul's PhD work and is highly practice-influenced. Derek's influence, as PhD supervisor, has been both as a colleague (we worked side by side over 30 years ago on a very large mixed-use construction project) and as an academic mentor with particular and serendipitous access to a wide range of literature through his credentials as active researcher, writer, and journal editor. We would like to describe ourselves as "pracademics," in the sense that we question practice through our reflection and we access many sources of literature from numerous disciplines.

We therefore frame this book as both an academic publication (reporting on cutting-edge research into project management) and a work, which we trust many practitioners (particularly those who reflect on project management practice and are open to alternative ways of seeing their world) will find pragmatic and useful. We strongly endorse the aims of research recently expressed from the rethinking project management network (Winter & Smith, 2006; Winter, Smith, Morris, & Cicmil, 2006)—in particular, the conception of project management as a social, rather than a purely instrumental, process—and we present our work to project managers as reflective practitioners rather than merely trained technicians. Our own personal values drive us to focus on how we see project management, so our view of the antecedents of project management best practices is shaped by those biases and worldviews.

The word "antecedent" is defined in the *New Oxford Dictionary of English* (Pearsall & Hanks, 2001) as "a thing or event that existed logically or logically precedes another" (p. 69). It is also defined in terms of "a person's parents" (p. 69). Therefore, we set this book's context in terms of being mindful of, and trying to explain, the conditions, worldviews, and provenance of project management practice. While we accept the dictionary definition of the term "antecedent," it appears to us somewhat incomplete. Parker, Williams, and Turner (2006) use the term in relation to proactive behavior at work and treat antecedents as causal factors. They argue that behavior is caused by antecedents, without which the intended effect (proactive behavior at work) will not take place. They also discuss distal antecedents as well as immediate antecedents, each of which may have the summative impact of providing a chain of events antecedent to the event or action. In a way, we can view antecedents as similar to predecessors in a critical path network diagram. In the next chapter, we will briefly discuss success factors and processes, which can be seen in part as antecedents. We are more interested in what needs to happen at the front end of projects, in terms of both actions/processes, as well as mindset, philosophy, or worldview of the purpose of projects for them to be deemed successful.

This book benefits from the contributions not only of the two co-authors but also of the extensive community of practice (CoP) of seasoned project management practitioners who added to the research rigor. Paul Steinfort's CoP is a wide group of colleagues, family members, friends, and past and present clients who share an interest in project management and in Paul's professional practice (PSA) and its outcomes. This work is substantially based upon the PhD thesis of one of the co-authors (Steinfort, 2010). Readers can access this thesis for a more extensive treatment of much of the actual data collected, which is contained in its appendices.[1] The other co-author, Derek Walker, took on the task of writing this book based upon his knowledge and experience as a project manager, an academic, and Paul Steinfort's PhD thesis supervisor. As the principal author in terms of physically writing this book, Derek has used and adapted large sections from Paul's thesis, with Paul's complete collaboration. The unnamed CoP members are gratefully acknowledged for their reflection and evaluation of outcomes reported in this book. The style of writing is intended to be accessible to both practitioners and project management scholars. As principal author, Derek will occasionally refer to Paul Steinfort by name (as Paul) and himself by name (as Derek) and will use the term "we" to mean Paul, Derek, and the CoP.

1.4 The Structure of This Book

The next chapter provides a literature review of those theoretical aspects that are relevant to the formulation of research questions and methods and for the analysis of findings from Paul's PhD research. As pragmatic methodological approaches are often seen as nontraditional, and as such questioned in some academic circles, we spend some time in our literature review justifying our research approach and our worldview rationale. It is important that readers understand our preferences and potential biases. The next chapter explains in detail our methodological approach, our research philosophy, and the points of view we take and what we understand as validity in terms of the evidence we provide and the justification and validation of our analysis of evidence. We then present some key and salient evidence from Paul's research. We follow that chapter with a discussion and analysis of the research findings and we present the model that we developed to encapsulate them. Finally, we complete the book with our conclusions and explanations of their implications.

1.5 Chapter Summary

This introductory chapter sets the scene for this book so that readers might know what to expect from it. We explained our view of the aim of projects, introducing terms such as "output," "outcome," "value," and "benefits." We firmly placed projects in a context of being within a coherent program management strategy that delivers beneficial outcomes through projects.

We then described this book both in terms of the journey that the co-authors have taken to write it and the context of aid relief projects. We completed the chapter by outlining the structure of the book.

---

[1]Go to URL link http://www.psaproject.com.au/ to access and download the entire thesis.

2

Literature Review

2.1 Chapter Introduction

In this chapter, we provide a literature review of those theoretical aspects that are relevant to the formulation of research questions and methods and for the analysis of findings from Paul's PhD research. We will present the relevant literature that we feel provides a necessary backdrop to the research reported upon. The main topics in the literature, each presented in a separate section, include a discussion of types of projects, success factors and processes, project to program management, aid project management techniques and leadership in terms of cultural context, stakeholder engagement and value, and authentic leadership. This is followed by a summary that reflects upon this chapter and establishes its link to Chapter 3.

2.2 Project Types

The debate surrounding the nature of project management, types of projects, and how they may differ or share characteristics has been a long one.

The move toward management by projects (Gareis,1989) adds greater complexity to that of earth project types because project management moves into spheres of business process re-engineering, change management or renewal projects (Andersen, 2006), and major business transformations (Arroyo, 2009; Arroyo & Walker, 2009). Projects are also seen as being critical drivers for organizational learning (Koskinen, 2009), and organizations are also observed establishing a project as a way of testing products, processes, or transformational ideas in ways that are highly innovative to the organization—so-called "vanguard" projects (Brady & Davies, 2004).

Project management work is also shown to be critical in managing project organization networks, working across projects within an organization, and managing business networks (Artto & Kujala, 2008). This notion of project business has led to the whole new view of projects being linked to, or independent from, their parent organization, where complex issues of autonomy and control are highly salient (Artto, Martinsuo, Dietrich & Kujala, 2008). Aid relief projects cross many organizational boundaries. They can involve a single nongovernment organiza-tion (NGO) or a cluster of them cooperating on a single program of projects, or the NGO may be coordinating numerous projects in a region. In the Aceh post-tsunami reconstruction effort, for example, many NGOs were managing projects for a range of donors to a range of communities on a wide range of initiatives. In many of these, the project management of these projects appeared chaotic, with shifting "rules" being applied by host countries. Often these "rules" did not exist, in the sense that the tsunami had destroyed whole communities along with their administrative infrastructures, so "rules" had to be devised on the spot. Here, cultural norms and regional traditions may have been substituted as goals and methods that could be adopted, so even the traditional earth project of building simple houses could end up being more like an air project in which everything appeared contestable.

These types of projects and ways of looking at how projects may be able to follow standard approaches and methodologies become highly contentious. If the project management world reverted to only viewing "real" projects as those referred to as earth projects, life would be much simpler. However, as shown above, life is not that simple. The implication of this view of the literature on project types for the aid reconstruction project context is that most of these projects are, in reality, highly complex—more complex than most traditional project managers are ever likely to face. In such circumstances, the use of standard project management tools and techniques can, as has been suggested by Atkinson (1999), be seen to be foolish or, as is suggested by Andersen (1996; 2008), even harmful when an unrealistic perspective of projects is taken.

Shenhar and Dvir (2004) have developed their novelty, complexity, technology, and pace (NCTP) project typology based on four dimensions that provide a visualization of the boundaries or the scope and scale of work to be undertaken and the required project management effort.

The first dimension is *novelty*. This is seen as ranging from *derivative* (where previously developed approaches, plans, methods, etc. can be applied routinely), through *platform* (where the project and its tasks are somewhat innovative, though they are based on, and adapted from, existing technology or processes), to *breakthrough* (where entirely new ways of thinking are required).

The second dimension is *complexity*. This is segregated into *assembly* (where the project entails putting together parts in a fairly routine manner), through *system* (where assemblies of resources and outputs from other assemblies are integrated), to *array* (where highly complex dispersed systems are brought together to achieve a common purpose).

Their third dimension is *technology*, which is categorized into *low-tech* (using well-tried and tested mature standard technology), *medium-tech* (using mostly mature technology, but with limited new technology or adaptations and the need to interface with some less mature technologies), *high-tech* (which uses as much new technology or significantly adapted mature technology as it does existing mature technology), and *super high-tech* (where technologies essentially do not exist at the project initiation and so have to be developed as the project proceeds).

Pace of project delivery is the final dimension, and it ranges from *regular* delivery time (where time pressure to deliver is generally standard), through *fast* or *competitive* (mostly for product to market situations, where the first of several competitors stands to gain significant enduring market share if it reaches the market first), to *blitz* or *critical* (where success or failure is totally dependent on reaching the market first and taking all rewards, or not).

A project involving re-housing in Aceh, which also involves associated civil engineering infrastructure and training locals in the use and maintenance of the facilities, could be seen to have the following characteristics:

- *Platform*, because it is based on similar projects undertaken by the NGO in similar situations. However, the allocated project management team would need to adapt standard practices and processes used elsewhere by the NGO.
- An *array*, because it involves a technical delivery of housing and associated physical infrastructure, but also cultural system interfaces due to local religious customs and beliefs, training and development interfaces, and perhaps dealing with severe trauma of the population.
- While a *low-tech* technical system may be used for standard housing and infrastructure, problems associated with construction in a devastated area may require considerable adaptation to meet local challenges.
- The *pace* may be intense due to the need to get the population housed and secure and living in as healthy a situation as can be achieved in the shortest possible time.

This project typology can be useful for mapping purposes and analysis to develop project delivery strategy (Shenhar & Dvir, 2004).

Söderlund (2005) conceptualizes a further typology of projects worth considering in terms of project management complexity and variety of project types. His typology comprises three project types—business, development, and change projects.

Business projects are those that lie at the core of an organization's purpose and are often the ones that result in an output—product and/or service—that is sold to clients. For construction companies this would be building buildings or infrastructure, and for NGOs it would mean getting on the ground to relieve communities and individuals to help them overcome some identified adversity.

Development projects are generally internally generated, and the consumer or market is the organization itself. These may be referred to as *initiatives*. For example, in engineering and construction firms, they may involve the development or extension of information communication technology (ICT) systems or educational and training programs, etc. For NGOs they may be similar in nature to those described for engineering and construction firms.

Change projects are those that transform the organization in some way and are usually directly linked to the organization's corporate strategy. They may include change management projects such as the cultural adaptation triggered by a merger or acquisition (Nogeste, 2010), or they may seek to align behaviors in some way or another. For NGOs, they may include projects where part of the recovery program involves transformational business opportunities for communities—e.g., through micro-financing by introducing new ways in which very small businesses can be developed through providing non-traditional financing to individuals to "bootstrap" small enterprise development.

These three project types may well co-exist within organizations. Some of them may not be recognized as projects by the organizations and so synergies of project experience may not be realized. Alternatively, each type may be recognized to the extent that inappropriately rigid common systems could be imposed.

We do not wish to imply that project management tools and techniques are inappropriate in most cases. What we have tried to stress in the above section, through our choice of cited literature, is that the focus of our study (aid disaster relief projects) indicates that traditional project management tools and techniques in and of themselves are not sufficient to deliver value. They must be used where pragmatically feasible, and we have already stressed our pragmatic view of project management and the world in general. Clearly there are times in most projects when stability and knowledge about the project context are clear and accessible and where project managers can therefore adopt systemized and standard (or easily adaptable) project management tools and techniques to deal with the projects as they would for an earth type project.

2.3 Success Factors and Success Processes—Antecedents

We start this section by considering our earlier definition of antecedents as causal factors or processes that combine in some way to have the summative impact of, and provide a chain of events that produces, a particular result or outcome. It is logical for us to consider the literature on the factors and processes of project success and failure.

An interesting set of questions presents itself. What are the underlying assumptions of the literature on project management success factors that may or may not apply to aid projects? What are some of the more problematic issues that aid projects face, which are significantly different from delivering, for example, commercial projects in difficult or distressing circumstances? How can we best approach the study of such projects? How can we summarize in a simple, but effective, universal framework the contextual project success constants and methods for application in any environment, particularly the project management framework application for undertaking Aid/Relief Projects (PMI, 2005)?

First we must consider the difference between project management success and project success. Baccarini (1999) suggests that successful project management delivers a project output that meets the project initiators' explicit expectations based on the project brief, whereas project success, as outlined in Section 1.2, delivers an outcome where the project output as an artifact contributes value toward the achievement of the goal that triggered the project.

Table 2-1 illustrates a study of success factors, which Hyväri (2006) gathered using a rigorous questionnaire completed by 25 experienced project managers in a range of industry sectors.

Early investigators of project management success include de Wit (1988), Pinto, and Slevin (1987), Finch (2003), and Delisle and Thomas (2002). Hyväri (2006) provides a useful comparison of the top 10 identified factors ranked by comparison, based upon both her study and other comparable studies. These were conducted in different parts of the world and in varying industry sectors adopting project management. It is interesting to note the variance in ranking, but there are close links and it is always difficult to truly compare rankings like this in a meta-study, because differently worded survey questions may mean similar things. For example, in Table 2-1 the top-ranked factor for three of the cited authorities was "Project Mission," whereas for Hyväri it was "Communication."

As Christenson (2007) and Christenson and Walker (2004) note, with respect to the pivotal importance of project vision, a vision must clearly state a project's

Table 2-1   Project Management Overall Ranked Success Factors: Source, Hyväri (2006, p. 38)

	This Study	Finch (PM) (2003)	Delisle & Thomas (2002)	Pinto & Prescott (1988)	Pinto & Slevin (1987)
A) Project mission	6	7	1	1	1
B) Top management support	4	6	9	7	2
C) Project schedule/plans	5	5	5	9	3
D) Client consultation	2	1	2	2	4
E) Personnel	9	10	10	10	5
F) Technical task	7	9	4	3	6
G) Client acceptance	3	4	6	4	7
H) Monitoring and feedback	10	3	3	5	8
I) Communication	1	2	8	6	9
J) Troubleshooting	7	8	7	8	10

Note: Numbers in this table indicate relative rankings of different factors in individual studies.

purpose and mission. Thus, communication of the project vision, mission, and goals is vital to its effective acceptance by project participants. So the importance of Table 2-2 lies not so much in its ranking of factors, but rather in its provision of a meta-study guidance of success factors that have been argued to strongly influence, if not cause, project management success. We can visualize these groups into sometimes overlapping clusters of factors.

Table 2-2   Project Management Ranked Success Factors by Project Phase: Source, Hyväri (2006, p. 38)

Project Implementation Profile by Phases				
	Definition	Planning and Organizing	Implementation and Control	Closeout
A) Project mission	1*	4*	10*	9*
B) Top management support	5	5*	4	4
C) Project schedule/plans	6	2	3*	7
D) Client consultation	2*	3	8*	3*
E) Personnel	8	7	6	10
F) Technical task	7	6	6*	8*
G) Client acceptance	4	8*	9	2
H) Monitoring and feedback	10	10	4	5
I) Communication	3	1	1	1
J) Troubleshooting	9	9	2*	6

Note: Numbers in this table indicate relative rankings of different factors by phases found in this study. Asterisks (*) indicate factors found important by Pinto & Prescott (1988).

These are *leadership* related factors (project mission, top management support, communication), *stakeholder engagement* factors (client consultation, communication, client acceptance), *technical expertise* factors (personnel, technical task, trouble-shooting) and operational *planning and control* factors (project schedule/plans, monitoring and feedback, trouble-shooting). These can be further conceptualized as front-end factors, operational factors, and management factors across project phases.

Our work has focused on antecedents to project management best practices, and while this is relevant to factors occurring during project execution, much of our interest lies at the front end of projects—initiation, planning, and project setup. This can also be seen as being affected by the processes used in project management and how they are applied from project initiation to completion, as indicated by Zwikael (2008) in Table 2-3.

Significantly, the top nine of these project management best practices are front-end processes which can be seen as antecedents of project management success. The literature provides substantial indications of likely antecedents to project management best practices, ranging across numerous industry sectors and coun-

Table 2-3   Recommendation for Top Project Management Best Practice Adoption: Source, Zwikael (2008, p. 400)

Critical Top Management Support Processes	Relevant Industries and Countries	Best Practices
Supportive project organizational structure	Engineering Production Government Israel New Zealand Japan	1. Pure project structure when projects are a significant share of organizational processes 2. Matrix organization in a complex and dynamic environment 3. Carefully define level of power for line managers verses project managers in matrix organizations
Existing project success measures	Engineering Production Israel	4. Define project success measures 5. Set project targets 6. Stakeholders to approve project targets
Refreshing project procedures	Engineering Production Japan	7. Frequently review project procedures with groups of project managers 8. Frequently update project management procedures
Organizational project quality management	Software Japan Israel	9. Establish a project excellence center 10. Involve the quality assurance department with project managers 11. Improve cooperation between these departments and project managers
Standard project management software	Engineering New Zealand Japan Israel	12. Decide upon a project management software program to use 13. Purchase the software 14. Train project managers on how to use the software 15. Involve the PMO in supporting project managers using the software
Organizational project resource planning	Software Israel Japan	16. Manage project shared resources on the organization or department level 17. use an intranet based project management software package

tries, and much of the literature cited here is based on survey data. This approach is useful for a meta-view of the project management best practice antecedents we were interested in identifying, but most of these studies lack the in-depth, fine-grained texture of the lived experience of project management team members who are responsible for success or failure.

This literature review did, however, provide a useful overview for us to frame our likely candidates for antecedents, and with which to later validate and analyze our research findings. Investigating the lived experience of project managers to explore more rich contextual issues has only recently been accepted as a valid way of studying project management success (Hodgson & Cicmil, 2006), as we will discuss in more depth in Section 2.5. It became evident from the literature review, more fully available in Paul Steinfort's thesis, that there is a gap in investigating project management success factors and processes from a lived experience point of view. Further, the literature cited above and more widely available appears to favor more traditional project management sectors such as construction and IT. Examples taken from the aid project sector are rare, as are examples from many emerging project management areas such as events, entertainment, business transformation through change, and business process re-engineering. It is clear that this field of study has much to reveal.

2.4 Project to Program Management—Front-end Importance

The relevance of this section to our topic is that important processes identified as critical in Section 2.3 happen at the front end of projects. There is an old Finnish saying, "well planned is half completed." Appreciating how simple, yet effective, the generic planning process is for all levels of the organization is the key to project management success. This highlights two important potential antecedents of project management success. One is for people involved in the project to understand the purpose and aim of a project and how it fits in with the expected benefit to be realized, and the other is how to plan for that to be realized.

The above literature suggests that understanding a project's purpose is a vital antecedent of project management success. This may be manifested by a well-articulated project vision, mission, and set of objectives, best developed from a clearly-constructed and well-framed business case that has been approved and supported through a rigorous filtering process. Many potential and quite different projects can be initiated to deliver an identified benefit.

The process used to prioritize and select projects within a program of discrete projects is a stage gate system. This is a critical part of program management (Pellegrinelli, 1997; Norrie, 2006; 2008; Office of Government Commerce, 2007; Thiry & Deguire, 2007; Levin & Green, 2008; PMI, 2008b; Artto, Martinsuo, Gemünden, & Murtoaro, 2009). Programs are the delivery vehicles for beneficial outcomes. In the aid relief project used in this book as one focus of study, the programs involved re-housing, and rebuilding livelihoods and lives, as well as helping to build a resilient community in Aceh, Indonesia. This raises two questions: Which option (project) should be delivered first, and which ones link in a kind of critical path (using a project management planning term that is well understood by project managers)?

The stage gate process can be a rigorous one in which project sponsors pit their potential projects against each other. This competitive struggle has the potential to force project business cases to be clearly enunciated, so that everyone is clear about how each project fits into the strategic goals of the organization in order to deliver an outcome that meets the needs of that organization. At the same time, this stage gate process is not without potential problems. Norrie (2006; 2008) cautions against taking a purely financial return on investment (ROI) standard for prioritizing projects, rather than considering the benefit objective and how it relates to the organization's strategic intent in pursuit of competitive advantage or business sustainability.

The aim of the project and program may be to positively impact on the organization's "customers" in order to sustain its existing business, or it may be to prepare the organization for the future so that it remains sustainable. This links to the wider view of success advocated by Shenhar, Dvir, Levy and Maltz (2001). Walker and Nogeste (2008) further adapt this view. Figure 2-1 illustrates another adaptation that indicates how success can be viewed through various lenses—the project lens, the customers' lens, the current and future business lenses, the project success lens, the program lens, the portfolio lens, and the organizational sustainability lens. Each can yield a different assessment of how successful a project may have been in contributing to the wider view of success.

Figure 2-1 suggests that maintaining a rigid ROI in stage gate minimum percentage rate, for example, can be detrimental to business success by privileging financial "success" rather than achieving a satisfied customer base that provides continued business. Further, it can inhibit experimentation and development of new

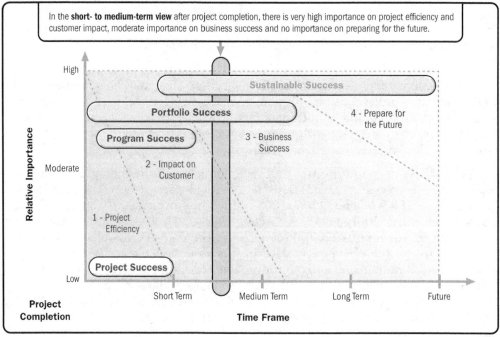

Figure 2-1   Success in Terms of Project, Program, Portfolio, and Sustainability

potential through vanguard projects (Brady & Davies, 2004), as discussed earlier. Projects need to fit into an organization's strategy, so clustering them into programs or projects makes sense. However, a further caution that has been raised about business cases used for screening or prioritizing projects is the problem of "strategic truth" (i.e., outright lies) about the costs and benefits of a project (Flyvbjerg, Holm, & Buhl, 2002; Flyvbjerg, Rothengatter, & Bruzelius, 2003).

A rigorously challenged and screened business case is vital for exposing potential misrepresentation of the aim and purpose of a project, as well as clarifying and promoting better understanding of its place in achieving an organization's strategic objectives. The stage gate process used for program and portfolio selection does not necessarily achieve this—though in theory it should (Cooper, Edgett, & Kleinschmidt, 1997; Archer & Ghasemzadeh, 1999; Cooper, 2005). However, continual and frequent evaluation of projects at stage gate reviews can serve as an effective process to challenging project assumptions and their continued validity. A danger is that once a project is approved and started it is very difficult to stop it, even if it becomes irrelevant. This is where a test of relevance is necessary to allow a project to proceed, when it is reviewed throughout its delivery as part of a project review process (Williams, 2007; Klakegg, Williams, Walker, Andersen & Magnussen, 2011). One tool, discussed in more detail in the next section, is the use of the logical framework used extensively in the aid project world but largely ignored in the general project management literature, except for a few papers (Baccarini, 1999; Crawford & Bryce, 2003).

Other important aspects of program and portfolio management are the roles of project sponsors, project management offices, and strong support for integrating projects into programs. Strong support by a project sponsor and senior management has been highlighted earlier as being an important project success factor and antecedent (Helm & Remington, 2005; Englund & Bucero, 2006). Crawford and Cooke-Davies (2006) argue that sponsors play a pivotal role in mediating between those who define organizational strategy and those who implement it through projects. These roles are crucial, and the people who perform them need to be convinced that the business case for a project is viable and achievable if they are to effectively champion it within situations where its purpose is questioned. They need to not only be genuinely, affectively committed (Meyer & Allen, 1991) to supporting the project, but also have the ability to effectively fight for and obtain the required resources, moral support, and other measures that will allow the project to continue. Strong sponsor support requires that the sponsor has the power and/or influence to ensure that the project is sustained (Englund & Bucero, 2006). Thus, the business case and value proposition must be clear to those providing support for it. An antecedent is therefore that the project vision or overarching aim must be clearly articulated and resonate with the aims and objectives of key stakeholders who can influence the political debate surrounding the project's survival and existence.

Project management offices (PMOs) are often required, as part of their remit, to provide a methodology or an organizational approach to managing projects, and to monitor and evaluate project performance. They are also often required to offer support, training, and knowledge transfer across projects and other tasks that help leverage expertise from project to project, program to program, and portfolio to portfolio within organizations (Office of Government Commerce, 2007; Aubry, Hobbs, & Thuillier, 2008; Cartwright & Walker, 2008). The role and function of a PMO, however they evolve over time, should lead to a logical system of governance, which confirms the need for viable projects as logical parts of a program, and ensure that these projects attract the necessary resources and political support to sustain them (Hobbs & Aubry, 2007; 2008; Cartwright & Walker, 2008).

This section has presented our literature review with a view to adopting a more holistic view of projects within programs and articulating how a rigorous stage gate review and a program management view can be useful for enhancing the chances of projects being relevant, valuable, and capable of delivering what is needed. We have also indicated how PMOs can be used to normalize project management practice across an organization so that best practice is understood and hopefully achieved. Front-end work entails ensuring that the "right" things are being done and that all parties to a project have been exposed to (and perhaps persuaded to believe in) the vision, mission, aims, and objectives of a project, so that the chance of their affective commitment to successfully delivering the project is embedded in project teams.

2.5 Rethinking Project Management

The Rethinking Project Management (RPM) initiative has influenced us in this book and in our work. The initiative emerged in the United Kingdom (UK) and involved a mix of academics and practitioners who shared an interest in project management. The purpose of the initiative was to link reflective practitioners and academics to enable them, through a range of conversations, to reframe what project management has to offer, how it is enacted, and what makes up its philosophical basis (Winter & Smith, 2006). While the RPM initiative was being undertaken, a parallel initiative—"making projects critical," in which projects are investigated to provide a fine-grained understanding of the lived experience of project team members—was being pursued, with several of the same academics included as part of both initiatives. The relevance of those initiatives to this research and findings is encapsulated in the objectives of both these initiatives because they both seek to uncover the lived experience of project management team members.

The agenda of the RPM has been summarized by the formulation of a series of new research directions which this group vowed to pursue:

1. From research on the life cycle model of projects and project management, to theories of complexity of project management
2. From projects as instrumental processes, to projects as social processes
3. From product creation as the prime focus, to value creation as the prime focus
4. From narrow conceptualization, to broader conceptualization of projects—having the need for new concepts and approaches to help facilitate this activity, particularly at the front end of projects
5. From practitioners as trained technicians, to practitioners as reflective practitioners

The research that we report on here falls squarely within all these research directions. Direction 5 is particularly salient, as this research took a highly pragmatic view—mainly because both co-authors have our formative experiences anchored in being project management practitioners, so naturally for us, the sense-making and workability aspects of validation are particularly important.

We argue that this research links in well with the RPM initiative, because we are also focusing our research on reflective practice based upon Paul's 40 years of diaries and reflections on his professional experience, added to the reflections of his extensive network of colleagues who form, for this research, a community of practice (CoP). Wenger, McDermott and Snyder (2002) define CoPs as "groups of people who share a concern, a set of problems, or a passion about a topic, and who deepen their knowledge and expertise in this area by interacting on an ongoing basis" (p. 4). Paul's CoP was instrumental in validation as well as in data gathering in terms of opinions, reflections, and analysis of data gathered through this study. Paul is CEO of a successful project management practice that has managed billions of dollars worth of projects, many of which were highly complex and socially sensitive while being of relatively low dollar "value" compared to other projects, such as in construction. Therefore, he has pursued the research reported on in this book as a practitioner, in order to make sense of its outcomes for practitioners. Thus, Direction 5 of the RPM initiative is very well addressed by this book.

2.6 Aid Project Management Approaches and Techniques

We discovered a number of techniques used by the aid project world that are not widely known or appreciated by the traditional project management world. We feel that bringing these to light to the project management world in general is a valuable contribution.

The academic literature available on aid/relief project management is not extensive and mostly recent. There are, however, wide-ranging and varying quality publications from aid agencies and global groups on methods and background of aid/relief project management, which mainly address practical methodology, methods, processes, and the tools to work with them (USAID, 1973; UNICEF, 1990; UNDP, 2002; 2003; ACFID, 2009; World Bank, 2004; AusAID, 2005; 2007).

Although there are several valuable journals on international development and a number of theses on a range of allied issues, there is little mainstream work specifically addressing aid/relief projects. The gap identified in project management practice, as it is currently evolving in the commercial project management world, is complemented by observations in the field of how aid projects function and by a growing body of literature that is critical of traditional project management techniques being applied in what may be viewed as inappropriate situations. This suggests that there is a range of project planning and performance measurement approaches better suited for ambiguous or poorly defined aid or social service delivery projects (Sigsgaard, 2002; Earle, 2003; Ramage & Armstrong, 2005).

There are some useful papers on international development project management in a more general sense, as distinct from post-disaster relief projects (Diallo & Thuillier, 2004; 2005; Ika, Diallo, & Thuillier, 2009). These address the cultural challenges, as well as success and project methodology, in particular instances. From a project management perspective, one good paper in this respect analyzes project management in Africa and specifically notes the "paucity in literature" written for project managers in developing countries (Muriithi & Crawford, 2003). Some research has also been conducted on project/construction management work looking at institutional/World Bank types of projects and both their methodologies and success factors (Baum, 1978; Long, Ogunlana, Quang, & Lam, 2004). However, there is indeed a paucity of literature in the field of disaster or post-disaster project management—hence, we have written this book.

A series of natural disasters followed the earthquakes and tsunamis that struck the Southeast Asia region on December 26, 2004, killing hundreds of thousands of people and leaving many more destitute and homeless. These tragic events have triggered a surge in interest in predictive and disaster response research and, to a lesser extent, in the improved delivery of critical aid relief projects. Among a range of institutions, PMI responded generously with a post-disaster rebuild methodology (PMI, 2005). This defines the intended scope, broad though it claims to be, but is nonetheless aimed at "rudimentary" projects, so one assumes that the kinds of major reconstruction projects principally involved after these two disasters may be excluded by this document. We do find some significant gaps in its applicability, perhaps due to its limited scope. The book's methodology is geared to responding to highly visible and tangible projects, such as those found in the construction, aerospace, and shipbuilding industries. We also raise questions about the assumption that post-disaster rectification activities (or rebuilds) can be deemed "projects." Post-disaster relief activities for major events such as the 2004 tsunami may well be better considered as being scalable programs of work.

Whitty and Schulz (2007) argue that this PMI methodology, and the whole *PMBOK® Guide*, in fact, is heavily influenced by a "Western" puritanical ideology, which views performance in terms of the "iron triangle" being of paramount concern. We know that the world has a broad range of ways by which people value "performance," and those cultural norms dominate perceptions of what is correct and proper (Hofstede, 1991; Trompenaars, 1993). Moreover, recent studies undertaken as part of the Global Leadership and Organizational Effectiveness (GLOBE) study (House, Javidan, Hanges, & Dorfman, 2002) also highlight marked differences between the way that Indonesians in Aceh, for example, would view the appropriateness of the behavior of project management team leaders and how U.S. or Australian project management teams, for example, would evaluate it.

Aid agencies are required to conform to stringent project reporting requirements in order to satisfy the wide range of stakeholders. Project monitoring and evaluation (M&E) information systems (IS), frequently a requirement for funding, are believed to inform the reporting process (Crawford & Bryce, 2003). The logical framework approach (LogFrame or LFA) is another tool widely used throughout the aid industry for project design and appraisal (Baccarini, 1999). Although much of the literature also promotes the use of LogFrame for the purposes of M&E, it has proven inadequate (Earle, 2003).

The following subsections will discuss LogFrame and M&E in more depth, as they are project management tools developed by the aid project world that could be used both effectively and to advantage in the project management world in general.

2.6.1 LogFrame

LogFrame provides a high level statement of goals, measures, and expected resources to do the work and base assumptions. AusAID (2005) states that

> Constructing the Activity Description in the matrix involves a detailed breakdown of the chain of causality in the activity design (and the associated means-ends relationships). This can be expressed as follows:
>
> - *if* inputs are provided, *then* the work program can be undertaken;
> - *if* the work program is undertaken, *then* outputs will be produced;
> - *if* outputs are produced, *then* component objectives will be achieved;
> - *if* component objectives are achieved, *then* the purpose will be supported; and;
> - *if* the activity purpose is supported, this should then contribute to the overall goal.
>
> Each level thus provides the rationale for the next level down: the goal helps justify the purpose, the purpose the component objectives, and so on down the hierarchy. (p. 3)

Jackson (1997) illustrates the iterative process in Figure 2-2.

Figure 2-2 shows that there is much justification built into LogFrame when properly and rigorously applied. The means-to-ends logical path works in both directions to illustrate assumptions about how each step is to be delivered, from the top of the hierarchical representation (the value or vision) to the specific tasks that need to be planned and executed. Also, it normally documents performance indicators as well as means of verification.

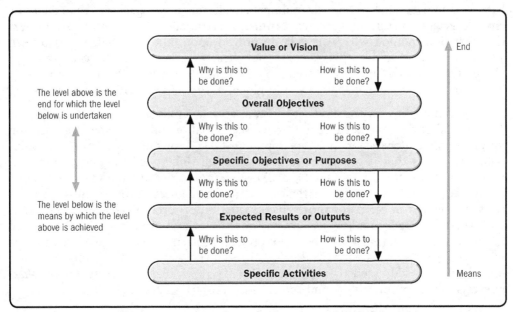

Figure 2-2   Logical Framework Approach (LogFrame): Source, Jackson (1997, p. 10)

Table 2-4   Logical Framework Approach Example: Source, AusAID (2005, p. 3)

Activity Description	Indicators	Means of Verification	Assumptions
Goal or Impact – The long term development impact (policy goal) that the activity contributes at a national or sectoral level	How the achievement will be measured – including appropriate targets (quantity, quality and time)	Sources of information on the Goal indicator(s) – including who will collect it and how often	
Purpose or Outcome – The medium term result(s) that the activity aims to achieve – in terms of benefits to target groups	How the achievement of the Purpose will be measured – including appropriate targets (quantity, quality and time)	Sources of information on the Purpose indicator(s) – including who will collect it and how often	Assumptions concerning the Purpose to Goal linkage
Component Objectives or Intermediate Results – This level in the objectives or results hierarchy can be used to provide a clear link between outputs and outcomes (particularly for larger multi-component activities)	How the achievement of the Component Objectives will be measured – including appropriate targets (quantity, quality and time)	Sources of information on the Component Objectives indicator(s) – including who will collect it and how often	Assumptions concerning the Component Objective to Output linkage
Outputs – The tangible products or services that the activity will deliver	How the achievement of the Outputs will be measured – including appropriate targets (quantity, quality and time)	Sources of information on the Output indicator(s) – including who will collect it and how often	Assumptions concerning the Output to Component Objective linkage
↑ **Work Program** (not usually included in the matrix itself)			

LogFrame typically follows a 4-by-4 matrix structure, as shown in Table 2-4. Each cell is described in the example provided and, as we can see, the schemata provide a rigorous front-end project planning instrument. At the very least, it offers the start of a method which may be improved upon, but one that has also been significantly accepted as being epistemologically sound in practice around the world and is possibly more accepted globally than PMI (PMI, 2008a) methodology. It certainly has extensive application in global aid/relief programs and projects.

LogFrame follows a process that includes both an analysis and a planning phase. At the head of the matrix in Table 2-4 we see "Goal or Impact." The Organisation for Economic Co-operation and Development (OECD) prime requirement of evaluation criteria is that it measures *relevance, effectiveness (or efficacy), efficiency, impact,* and *sustainability* (OECD, 2007). Therefore, the indicators to be used and the means of evidence-based verification, through the M&E process, must be critically considered in terms of those five evaluation criteria. This logic aligns well with the more traditional project management views of project success discussed in Section 2.3 and forms a solid basis for project front-end selection at stage gates, as well as continual monitoring (Klakegg, 2010). The LogFrame analysis phase follows four iteratively addressed themes (AusAID, 2005): *problem analysis, stakeholder analysis, objectives analysis,* and *selection of a preferred strategy.*

Problem analysis can use techniques such as cause-and-effect mapping. This is frequently used in total quality management (TQM) approaches in which a fishbone-like figure is developed, with the head indicating the most visual effect and the "bones" linked to the fish "spine" representing potential causes. These maps can then be used to construct a problem breakdown structure, or problem tree (AusAID, 2005). *Stakeholder analysis* is now coming to be seen as a more important part of project management (Overseas Development Administration, 1995; Winch, 2004; Bourne & Walker, 2006; PMI, 2008a; Bourne, 2009). Various tools are available to produce a visualization of stakeholder influence—e.g., the Stakeholder Circle™ (Bourne & Walker, 2005; Bourne, 2009). *Objectives analysis* can use the standard project management practice of objectives breakdown structure (OBS), which looks very similar to developing a work breakdown structure (Bachy & Hameri, 1997). *Selection of a preferred strategy* follows a range of option and priority choice approaches, including a stage gate decision-making approach (Office of Government Commerce, 2007) or other suitable decision-making methodologies. The planning phase can follow standard project management practices.

LogFrame clearly has extensive application in aid/relief programs and projects. It also addresses some of the likely antecedents of project management practice in this area, and in fact each of our key research partners in developing Paul's soft systems methodology (SSM) rich pictures was also familiar with the LogFrame application, including its limitations. The *PMBOK® Guide* does not have this more open, front-end stance to projects, although more recently it has attempted to resolve this through adding both program and portfolio standards applicable for the front-end and evaluation of projects. The *PMBOK® Guide* suffers from some recognized rigidity regarding its application in the actual transfer through the life cycles of the projects, but these can be addressed as part of the possible solution and the synergizing with traditional project management, evaluation theory, SSM, and action research. (See Chapter 3 for more on these research approaches.)

LogFrame has attracted some criticism. Jackson (1997), for example, cites at least four weaknesses of the approach:

1. It frequently produces poor results, because any initial negative focus pervades the rest of the LogFrame process. This often results in limited vision of potential solutions. This negativity can be due to:
   - Dealing with cultures that consider it inappropriate to openly discuss problems or to criticize others
   - Not being suited to situations where there is a lot of uncertainty or disagreement about what constitutes the main problem
   - Assumptions being made about the nature of the problems that can be readily determined at the beginning of the planning process. This inhibits an exploratory style where learning from experience can take place.
2. It is often rigid in both its development and its practice, which can inhibit and suppress innovative thinking and adaptive management.
3. It is often developed after the project has been designed, rather than being used as the basis for design. Its use late in the design process can often be attributed first to a lack of understanding of its purpose and use, and second to it being forced on NGOs by funding agencies as their control mechanism rather than as a design and scoping management tool.
4. It is not suitable for monitoring unintended consequences and is therefore rarely considered adequate as a key planning tool. (p. 4)

It becomes clear that there are different types of projects with very different needs and demands upon them, and very different characteristics, yet professional bodies continue to assume that a one-size-fits-all approach is appropriate—e.g., PMI with the *PMBOK® Guide* (PMI, 2008a) —or, in many of the aid projects, the logical framework approach.

2.6.2 Results-Based Management—Monitoring and Evaluation (M&E)

Throughout the delivery and actualization of projects, there needs to be a governance structure in place which provides the means to check whether intended results are actually being achieved. This involves a process where transparency and accountability are vital. The term "governance," which has more recently entered the project management lexicon, is derived from the corporate governance literature (Davis, Schoorman, & Donaldson, 1997; Jones, Hesterly, & Borgatti, 1997). We have seen the term used in a project management context relatively recently (Turner & Keegan, 2001; Winch, 2001; Miller & Hobbs, 2005; Crawford & Cooke-Davies, 2006; PMI, 2006b; Müller, 2009). Walker, Segon, and Rowlinson (2008) state that

> The term "corporate governance" can sound very grand and intimidating but in essence it can be seen as setting reasonable, acceptable (ethical) rules and regulations that protect those who have a stake in a project, including supply chain and team member participants. It is about accountability and response—who does what, under what rules and for what rationale. Further, it revolves around structures being in place to facilitate accountability and secondly it requires the will and capacity to ensure that governance structures are effective in ensuring ethical standards are in place. (pp. 126–127)

Much of this accountability and establishment of a robust priority-setting process at the front end of any project, and then an M&E process to support accountability, fall under the realm of project governance. The situation for more standard project management situations has been recently researched (Williams, 2007; Klakegg et al., 2011), with Figure 2-3 illustrating the processes used to provide good project management governance.

Auditing and reporting facilitates openness for accountability and transparency. The common vehicles are ad hoc reports, regular reporting, and special purpose reports and reviews. The situation in the aid project world is similar and institutionalized.

Results-Based Management, also referred to as Performance Management, is best defined in a comprehensive report by the Development Assistance Committee (DAC) Working Party on Aid Evaluation (Binnendijk, 2000) as a broad management strategy aimed at achieving important changes in the way project agencies operate, with improving performance on projects (achieving better results) as the central orientation. The development cooperation (or donor) agencies whose experiences were reviewed included USAID, DFID, AusAID, CIDA, Danida, the UNDP, and The World Bank. Results-Based Management with performance measurement is the process an organization follows to objectively measure how well its stated objectives are being met.

This same document also addresses how to enable the effective incorporation of LogFrame and Risk Management into Results-Based Management, while at the same time keeping a critical eye on their limitations. It concludes by point-

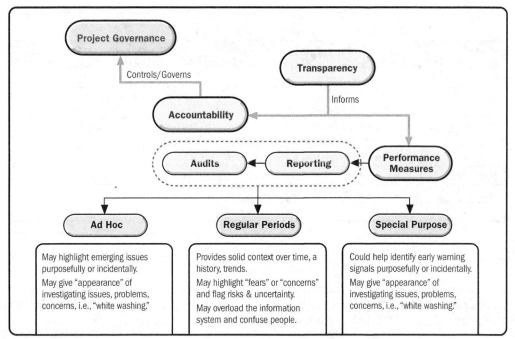

Figure 2-3   A Governance Framework for Reviewing Projects: Source, Klakegg et al. (2011, forthcoming)

ing out that the challenge is to balance project performance monitoring needs at all LogFrame hierarchy levels, without overburdening the monitoring system or having it displace evaluation or implementation activities. The related factor here is also that most NGO/aid agencies are typically under-resourced and under-trained in project management or measurement of any critical form.

The cornerstone of M&E in Results-Based Management is to have clear and transparent means of verifying performance indicators, as illustrated in Table 2-4. Binnendijk (2000) states that performance measurement at the project level is concerned with both *measuring a project's implementation progress* and *measuring achieved results*.

> These two broad types of project performance measurement might be distinguished as (1) implementation measurement which is concerned with whether project inputs (financial, human and material resources) and activities (tasks, processes) are in compliance with design budgets, workplans, and schedules, and (2) results measurement which focuses on the achievement of project objectives (i.e., whether actual results are achieved as planned or targeted). Results are usually measured at three levels—immediate outputs, intermediate outcomes and long-term impacts. (p. 15)

Project performance indicators are established to flag progress toward a goal, outcome, or output. They can be lagging indicators such as resources consumed, but these only tell us what has happened in the past. Leading indicators, by contrast, predict the future, given certain assumptions. For example, team satisfaction may

Table 2-5   Criteria for Sound Performance Indicators: Sources, Kusek and Rist (2004, p. 68) and Jackson (1997, p. 13)

Criterion	Description
Clear	Precise and unambiguous (Kusek & Rist)
Relevant	Appropriate to the subject at hand (Kusek & Rist) and accurate to be able to reflect what is intended to be measured (Jackson)
Economic	Available at a reasonable cost (Kusek & Rist) and feasible in terms of available resources to monitor and evaluate (Jackson)
Adequate	Provide a sufficient basis to assess performance (Kusek & Rist)
Monitorable	Amenable to independent validation (Kusek & Rist) and able to be measured (Jackson)
Timely	To provide information when needed in a timely manner (Jackson)
Sensitive	To be able to detect subtle and significant changes over time (Jackson)

indicate current commitment, which may in turn indicate future level of effort applied. Table 2-5 illustrates the criteria for performance indicators based upon Kusek and Rist's (2004) CREAM typology and Jackson's approach (1997).

The focus on indicators is to monitor and evaluate on the basis of five considerations (Klakegg, 2010). First, *efficiency* relates to how well the project performs in terms of its project management success during the project delivery phase. Second, *effectiveness* is considered in terms of project front-end consideration as to how well the outcome will meet the purpose of the project, as well as the operation of the outcome of the project. Third, *impact* is relevant at both the front end, to ensure that the right measures are being used, and during the operational phase, to ensure that trends are effectively identified and tracked so that they are useful for predicting the expected effect of a trend that has been monitored. Fourth, *relevance*, as noted in Table 2-5, is important for the reasons described; this is vital for M&E both at the front end and during operational phases. Fifth, M&E must be *sustainable* at the front-end phase, during project delivery, and at the operational phase of the outcome.

2.6.3   Subsection Summary

We have described some of the more relevant techniques and approaches used in the aid project world, which we believe the traditional project management world would find interesting and valuable to consider. We consciously stressed how Log-Frame and M&E, when linked as part of Results-Based Management, share conceptual and pragmatic similarities. We showed how LogFrame can be compared to, and provide valuable insights into, the front-end planning of programs of projects. We explained, in summary, how it is used and provided authorities, which readers can consult to find more practical information about its use and limitations. Similarly, M&E shares much common ground with project monitoring and control. The five OECD criteria for evaluation—*relevance, effectiveness* (or *efficacy*), *efficiency, impact,* and *sustainability*—actually link in well with the success debate illustrated in Figure 2-1, which was adapted from Shenhar et al. (2001).

2.7 Leadership Issues

While it is useful to have a conceptual framework within which to plan and evaluate programs of projects in both the aid and traditional project management worlds, the enactment part of realizing best practice delivery from best processes requires a special and rigorous level of leadership.

Leading project delivery is a highly complex matter, even for so-called simple or low cost projects. In Section 2.1 we discussed project types and highlighted a trend toward product and services increasingly being bundled together as deliverables. We also suggested that aid projects are often situated in places where cultural and religious conditions are very different from those underpinning the traditional project management mindset, which Whitty and Schulz (2007) describe as highly puritanical in its roots. Sections 2.5 and 2.6 introduced the importance of engagement with stakeholders as a fundamental duty of project managers. This all requires a shift away from an overall "command and control" leadership style to one that better deals with highly complex situations, extreme turbulence, and much uncertainty.

2.7.1 Leading in Complex Situations and Environments

"Complexity" means many different things to many people. Baccarini's (1996) early definitions and discussions on complexity are probably the most frequently cited. He saw complexity in terms of dealing with the paradox of simultaneous differentiation and integration across a range of dimensions, such as the organizational and technological ones—i.e., complexity centers on dependency and interdependency. Jaafari (2003) took these ideas a step forward by identifying project management work in terms of a systems point of view, where the project is bounded in one sense, but is influenced by, and interacts with, a range of systems. He sees project environments as exhibiting characteristics of chaos and ambiguity, so that project managers need to respond to the world using a repertoire of behaviors. Jaafari also argues that there are fair degrees of self-organizing behaviors happening in many projects, which directly conflict with the "command and control" approach favored by many traditional project managers. Project managers need to cope with the paradox of dealing with organic action from self-organizing groups who exhibit something akin to "swarm intelligence" behaviors (Bonabeau & Meyer, 2001; Anderson & McMillan, 2003), where they get on with tasks seemingly undirected, yet highly purposeful and adhering to overall project goals. These goals may be established through highly prescriptive bureaucratic control, governed by strict adherence to rules and protocols.

Remington and Pollack (2007) more recently discuss how structural, technical, directional, and temporal complexity can be coped with, and they offer tools that may be used by project leaders. Williams, Eden, Ackermann, and Tait (1995) also demonstrate how systems' dynamic tools can be effectively used to map events, and responses to them, in complex settings. These tools can be used by project leaders for visualizing complex situations at the planning stage, or later as forensic evaluation tools. Williams later studied the detection of early warning signals (in Klakegg et al., 2011) and dealing with uncertainty, particularly from the front end of projects (Williams, 1999; Williams, Samset, & Sunnevåg, 2009; Williams, Klakegg, Magnussen, & Glasspool, 2010).

Schein (1996) also raises the issue of subcultures within organizations. He discusses differences in worldview, as well as approaches and responses to various dilemmas faced by a range of employee levels—technical or operator, engineering and executive. There is often much misunderstanding between subculture groups about a variety of issues because of their very different histories and backgrounds. This is explained by the formation of clans and their respective rituals (Smith, 2007; Smith & Winter, 2010). Numerous forces within organizations shape the reality of projects, and the cultural dimension of national prevailing cultures and subcultures of clans within projects. Also, external stakeholders tend to impose an often hidden, but critical, dynamic on the complexity of all projects. Dealing proactively using this form of leadership style is what Smith calls *project crafting.*

What we discovered through our research for this book was that aid project leadership within this complex dynamic requires many of the approaches suitable for complex or chaotic project contexts. Therefore, there is a need for much probing and testing action, which is then reflected upon in order to make sense of what appears to be happening, so that plans can move forward or be reframed or adjusted in some way. This forms a core concept of our empirical work (discussed later) because it validates a view of project management as a form of action learning. We have both experienced, within many traditional project management projects, a lot of activity involved in creating environments and experiments, which allow patterns to emerge; planning is undertaken on milestone priorities for the medium to long term, while detailed plans are only produced for the short term as is recommended (Andersen, Grude, & Haug, 1995). This uses what Andersen (2008) describes as *entrained thinking*—matching the flow of decision making and action to the natural pace of the environment in which that work takes place. This reinforces the need for leaders to be pragmatic and flexible in their leadership style and approach. It also requires high levels of emotional intelligence quotient (EQ) (Goleman, 1995; 1999; 2000; Clarke & Howell, 2009). An interesting finding by Turner, Muller, and Dulewicz (2009) is that:

> managerial and intellectual competencies are of primary importance for leaders of projects while emotional competencies become more important when gaining the commitment of followers in the team. It supports the assertion of Goleman (Goleman, Boyatzis, & McKee, 2002) that increasing EQ capability is required at higher levels of general management. These findings are likely to be relevant to anyone involved in selecting or developing project managers. (p. 212)

We have discussed stakeholders a number of times in this chapter and section. What or who are stakeholders? One definition comes from a consideration of agency theory, ethics, and both instrumental and convergent stakeholder theory (Donaldson & Preston, 1995; Jones & Wicks, 1999; Carroll & Buchholtz, 2000). Stakeholders are those who feel they have an interest, or some aspect of rights or ownership, in a project (Walker, Bourne, & Rowlinson, 2008). Clearly, there are many voiceless or invisible stakeholders in aid projects, such as those communities left devastated in the aftermath of disasters like the 2004 tsunami. Commonly, in disaster aid relief projects there is a palpable need for project managers to grapple with many competing demands from a wide range of stakeholders. These may be spoken, or if not, often obviously visible. The qualities and competencies demanded of project managers in this context are predominantly the so-called soft skills and competencies (Dainty,

Cheng, & Moore, 2004; Dainty, Bryman, Price, Greasley, Soetanto, & King, 2005) that largely constitute EQ. These revolve around empathy and self knowledge, the ability to see situations from the points of view of "others."

Stakeholder management involves a two-stage process. The first involves identifying stakeholders and understanding their potential influence and impact, which can be done using influence mapping or other visualization tools (Turner & Simister, 2000; Winch, 2004; Bourne & Walker, 2005; Olander & Landin, 2005; Aaltonen, Jaakko, & Tuomas, 2008; Smyth, 2008). The second stage involves developing an engagement plan, which includes identifying how to reinforce support, reduce opposition, and, most importantly, understand the basis of both support and opposition. In this way, the project manager can modify plans and priorities, either to suit a new understanding of "reality" or to frame a convincing message that influences stakeholders in some way. Finally, this is a valid project management process that requires a subproject all its own (Bourne, 2009).

To summarize, there is a strong potential cultural complexity that project managers from all types of projects may face and need to cope with. Cultural complexity can be a result of nationally-based sets of underlying assumptions and ways of working, emerging from project-external stakeholders or from project-internal cross-national team members. Cultural complexity can result from the clan and tribal cultural influences of subcultures within projects and stakeholder groups. Stakeholder engagement is vital, because both internal and external project stakeholders have the potential to render a project more or less complex, depending on which actions they take or instigate.

The final piece in the jigsaw puzzle we have tackled in this chapter is a consideration of how the leadership styles that are required to deal with the complex environment of aid relief projects may be applied to more traditional project management arenas. This discussion follows in the next subsection.

2.7.2 Leadership Style

We have argued thus far that an appropriate leadership style for complex projects requires empathy, flexibility, and a pragmatic approach. Also, where well-identified objectives and methods are known (either for the project as a whole, or for part of a more complicated or complex project), a more logical decision-making and guidance-oriented project management approach may be appropriate. What, then, does the literature offer about the leadership styles and qualities needed for the levels of complexity discussed in the Snowden and Boone (2007) complexity model?

Many leadership style scholars recommend that leaders have a repertoire of styles that they can apply in various situations (Thite, 1999; Goleman, 2000; Turner & Müller, 2005; Müller & Turner, 2007; Turner et al., 2009). Hersey, Blanchard and Johnson (1996) offered a four leadership style approach, based upon a *task guidance* and *relationship support* dimension, by also linking to what they call *job maturity* (ability) and *follower maturity* (willingness).

Style 1 (the "telling" style) is high task and low relationship oriented. It is suitable for followers who have low ability and perhaps low willingness to work on their own initiative and require high levels of follower supervision.

Style 2 (the "selling" style) relates to high task and high relationship levels. Decisions are explained to followers, giving them the opportunity to clarify instructions.

Style 3 (the "participating" style) is suitable for high relationship support and low task guidance. It is characterized by shared ideas and joint problem-solving discussion and is appropriate where both ability and willingness are high.

Style 4 (the "delegating" style) is characterized by low relationship support and low task guidance. An outline of the task requirement is given and followers have the power to choose how they perform the task.

This approach provides a promising categorization of leadership style by task complexity and follower ability and willingness.

A *transformational* leadership style described by Avolio (1996) and Bass (1985), appears more proactive. This style has also been proposed by Keegan and Den Hartog (2004) for a project management context in less ordered and more unordered contexts. It can be valuable in promoting an effective project vision with which to take a more flexible and evolutionary approach to developing plans and action, consistent with the use of Agile project management techniques and improvisation to deal with high levels of uncertainty, as described in Section 2.7.1.

The business literature also offers a great deal about leadership, which is relevant here. Leadership characteristics described as being highly inspiring or charismatic are admired by numerous scholars (for example, Wang, Chou, and Jiang, 2005), though their measures of charisma have much to do with the high trust and confidence of followers, based on benign behavior and perceived ability. Others feel that such leaders are suited to contexts where "there is a high anxiety level, conditions of crisis and change that intensify processes of projection, transference and attribution" (Popper & Zakkai, 1994, p. 7). This may be seen as ideal in the highly complex or chaotic contexts found in many aid relief or complex traditional project management projects. However, other scholars caution against being duped by charismatic leaders because of their tendency to be manipulative, shallow, or even Machiavellian—such leaders are often described as being narcissistic (Maccoby, 2000). Narcissism is a negative leadership trait, as the leader is seen as being self-serving, which often results in followers unquestioningly taking a course of action without understanding its potential consequences (Maccoby).

While charisma is seen as being inspirational, but at the same time a potentially limiting trait on its own, it has also been seen as a hallmark of transformational leaders. Avolio and Bass (1995) focus on *individual consideration* as the key one of the four "I"s that characterizes a transformational leadership style. These four "I"s (Avolio, 1996) are:

Idealized influence, by gaining trust, respect, and confidence through setting high standards of conduct and being a role model;

Inspirational motivation (similar in many ways to being charismatic), by articulating the future desired state (a vision) and a plan to achieving it;

Intellectual stimulation, through questioning the status quo and continuously innovating, even at the peak of success; and

Individual consideration, by energizing people to develop and achieve their full performance potential.

This transformation style has been variously refined, with different writers citing the importance of traits such as humility (Collins, 2001), and servant leadership or stewardship (Davis et al., 1997; Turner & Keegan, 2001; Christenson & Walker, 2003; Bluedorn & Waller, 2006), where leaders see themselves as being facilitators and supporters for the productive actions of others (Avolio, Gardner, Walumbwa, & May, 2004). This has led to the ideas of Avolio and Gardner (2005) about *authentic leadership*, which appear to be appropriate for the kinds of unordered contexts described in Snowden and Boone (2007).

A recent paper on authentic leadership in the context of construction sector project management (Toor & Ofori, 2007) attracted our attention as a good point of departure to explore how authentic leadership may apply not only to the construction project management sector, but also to other project management areas. Toor and Ofori provide a sound general review of some of the extensive and important literature relevant to their paper, and readers may wish to refer to that paper for a broader discussion of leadership styles particularly relevant to construction project management. Another paper that discusses authentic leadership, and also provides advice on how a capability maturity model can be used to measure authentic leadership, was recently published (Lloyd-Walker & Walker, 2010) and demonstrates that authentic leadership in project management can be measured and evaluated.

Avolio and others extended the final "I" in their transformational model into the concept of authentic leadership (Avolio & Bass, 1995; Avolio & Locke, 2002; Avolio et al., 2004; Avolio & Gardner, 2005; Avolio & Luthans, 2006). George, Sims, McLean, and Mayer (2007) state that:

> Authentic leaders demonstrate a passion for their purpose, practice their values consistently, and lead with their hearts as well as their heads. They establish long-term, meaningful relationships and have the self-discipline to get results. They know who they are. (p. 130)

At the core of this view of leadership behavior is consistency between espoused practice and practice in action. Key elements of the Avolio et al. (2004) model of authentic leadership behaviors and espoused values also include hope, trust, and positive emotions.

Followers identify with their leaders at both a personal and social level through their demonstrated hope, trust, and positive emotions. This, in turn, can influence followers' optimism and generate commitment, job satisfaction, meaningfulness, and engagement. The expected outcome of this is productive follower behaviors. Authentic leadership, according to the Avolio et al. (2004) model requires leaders who have confidence, optimism, hope, self-efficacy, and resilience (Luthans & Youssef, 2004). Leaders are aware of how they think and act, true to themselves, and are also aware of how they are perceived by others. Self-awareness and awareness of others are recurring themes within authentic leadership.

Authentic leaders are clear about their own values and moral perspectives, knowledge, and strengths and equally aware of these attributes within others. They are confident and hold a positive view of the future; they are resilient, perceived by others to be of high moral character, and they place a high importance on the development of employees as leaders. As a result, they lead from their own personal point of view (Shamir & Eilam, 2005). This is also consistent with the concept of emotional intelligence and the need for project managers to have not only good general intelligence but also managerial competencies and intelligence as well as emotional intelligence. These attributes allow them to select an appropriate leadership style based on context and their perception of the most effective way that their team responds to leadership style (Müller & Turner, 2007).

In this brief overview of leadership styles, we have identified how style and the degree of complexity of project context may be linked. We argued that, while transactional styles may be appropriate in more ordered contexts, they may result in continuance or normative commitment rather than affective commitment. Drawing upon the research and recommendations of Snowden and Boone (2007) about the leader's job, the danger signals to be aware of, and the actions that leaders should take to obviate those dangers, we also argued that transformation leadership can be effective in unordered contexts. Finally, in explaining the relevance of the term *authentic leadership*, we highlighted the views of George et al. (2007), who stress that true transformational leaders are true to themselves and thus provide a sound role model to followers (team members and other stakeholders). In drawing upon the Snowden and Boone (2007) model of ordered and unordered contexts, we explored the link between preferred leadership behaviors and styles, and project context.

2.8 Chapter Summary

This chapter provides a review of the literature relevant to understanding the antecedents of project management best practice, and in particular the lessons that can be learned from aid relief projects.

We began by outlining project types to better articulate the nature of the contexts facing project managers. Theories we found useful for this purpose included the project typology based upon a goals and methods matrix by Turner and Cochrane (1993); the Shenhar and Dvir (2004) NCTP model based on novelty, complexity, technology, and pace; and the topology of projects categorized into business, development, and change projects (Söderlund, 2005). These theories help us gain a more robust and holistic understanding of the types of projects that project managers are faced with, and therefore what practices may be adopted to best manage these projects in the various contexts in which they arise.

We briefly discussed success factors, in order to indicate the basis upon which project management best practice and project success may be judged. This led to a need to explore how the front end of projects and program management may be critical to project management and project success.

We then examined the rethinking project management literature, because the research reported on here involved deep reflection on the nature of project management and project success.

Our section on aid and project management approaches and techniques set the scene for the lessons that traditional project management literature can learn from the aid project world. Our focus was on LogFrame and Results-Based Management, through monitoring and evaluation as techniques that are suitable candidates for greater use in both ordered and highly unordered contexts.

Finally, in drawing these literature themes together in a pragmatic way, we discussed the leadership issues that project managers face and have to respond to. These themes included investigating the literature relating to ordered and unordered project contexts, the potential impact of national and organizational subcultural influences in leading teams and responding to external stakeholders, and, finally, the leadership styles that may be best suited to the complex contexts that are becoming more the norm for most projects today.

3

Research Methodology

3.1 Chapter Introduction

The purpose of this chapter is to explain available options to undertake the research reported upon in this book, to identify the approach chosen, and to justify our decision. We will describe in detail in a later chapter how the chosen research approach was undertaken. We assert that one of the benefits of Paul Steinfort's PhD study is that it strongly addresses the very issues that the rethinking project management groups have called for. To reiterate, the research directions that were proposed by Winter et al. (2006) are:

1. From research on the life cycle model of projects and project management to theories of complexity of project management
2. From projects as instrumental processes to projects as social processes
3. From product creation as the prime focus to value creation as the prime focus
4. From narrow conceptualization to broader conceptualization of projects—creating the needs for new concepts and approaches to help facilitate this activity, particularly at the front-end of projects
5. From practitioners as trained technicians to practitioners as reflective practitioners (p. 642)

Chapter 2 provided a literature review that framed our conceptualization of the research work reported upon in this book. Theories of complexity served as a useful starting point. The focus on people interaction is very much in line with research direction 2 above. The research direction and value creation relate to best practice in delivering project management value to stakeholders, as well as focusing on learning from the experience of aid relief project management. Section 2.4 specifically discussed the importance of the front end of projects to project management research. Finally, Paul's entire research thesis was predicated upon a pragmatic way of investigating and analyzing project management best practices, and his research approach completely embraced reflective learning, action research, and making a research contribution based on practice. Thus, it will be shown that the philosophical position we take for our research is one of pragmatism, praxis, and reflective learning through a series of action learning loops.

This chapter first explains, clarifies, and justifies our philosophical stance and the worldview (our ontology) we share relating to the reality of projects and the way we see the validity of the evidence (epistemology) that we present. We follow this section with a description of the research methodology that was followed, and we then present a section, which explains in more detail how Paul approached the research for the study results, which will be discussed at length and in depth in the following chapter. This chapter will conclude with a chapter summary.

3.2 Philosophical Stance, Ontology, and Epistemology

The purpose of the kind of research we undertook (addressing pragmatic practitioner-oriented problems) was to better understand a project management practice, situation, or problem in order to recommend action that could be taken to remedy it. The problematic situation was how to improve the chances of project success through the adoption of project management best practices. We aimed to enhance our understanding of project management best practices through: review of the relevant literature, reflection on over 40 years of Paul's diaries of project management practical experience, and empirical research on aid disaster relief projects as the lens through which we could study the phenomenon of "project management best practice." We chose aid relief projects as our empirical focus mainly because they are highly complex social projects and current trends suggest that project management is becoming more a matter of managing social situations than addressing purely technical situations. Our worldview is therefore framed by our practical experience of having been engaged in and managing many projects of varying types over many decades, which leads us to naturally favoring a pragmatic approach.

3.2.1 Philosophical Stance

Carr (2006) states that "in ancient Greece the word 'philosophy' referred to virtually all forms of serious intellectual inquiry and its modern separation from 'science' would make little sense" (p. 425). Literally, the meaning of philosophy is love of wisdom, knowledge, and truth. We first explain our way of seeing "truth" so that readers can be aware of any inherent bias and limitations to findings that our chosen research approach and way of seeing the work may impose on that work.

Eikeland (2007) provides a rigorous account of the evolution of philosophical thought and science, with detailed descriptions of the sources of many of the terms used in research today (see Table 3-1). He presents seven "ways of knowing," which provide us with some insights into the Greek origins, and more subtle meanings, of

Table 3-1   Aristotelian Ways of Knowing: Source, Eikeland (2007, p. 348)

Basis	Way of Knowing	Associated Rationality	English Equivalent
Aísthèsis (perception)	Theôrêsis = $zepistêmê_2$	Deduction, demonstration, didactics	Spectator speculation
	Páthos	??	Being affected passively from the outside
Empeiría (practically acquired experience)	Khrêsis Poíêsis Praxis$_2$	Tékhnê (calculation) Phrónêsis (deliberation)	Using Making, manipulating Doing: virtuous performance
	Praxis$_1$	Dialectics/dialogue. The way from novice to expert, from tacit to articulate	Practice, training for competence development and insight (theôría)
	Theôría = epistêmê$_1$	Dialogue, deduction, deliberation	Insight

the terms associated with philosophy and research, which frame the way we justify our understanding of "truth" and how we argue this to be acceptable and workable.

The first way of knowing is *theôrêsis*, which is based on perception and can be roughly equated to speculation by an observer, which is rationalized by deduction and demonstration of didactics, i.e., through teaching. This way of knowing fits in well with the concepts of mentoring and coaching and also situational learning. Paul's professional project management practice (PSA), of which he is chief executive officer (CEO), is particularly focused on developing his staff and his client base through mentoring and coaching. Paul has been pursuing this style of project management for almost two decades and his practice's business plan is very much based on this foundation. This approach offers advantages to both mentor and mentee or protégé, coach, and coached (Mullen & Noe, 1999), as it fosters a process of co-learning. Each party opens its ideas to be challenged and reframed, so joint learning takes place. Another form of this kind of learning evolves through workplace situational learning (Lave & Wenger, 1991) and has been recently shown to be very effective in a project management context (Sense, 2005; 2007).

Two other ways of knowing (from Table 3-1) are related to practically acquired knowledge through experience in differing forms. *Khrêsis* is defined as a way of knowing which, along with the other terms we will explain in this section, is based on empirical evidence practically acquired through experience. Khrêsis is associated with calculation and the English equivalent terms are associated with *using*. *Poíêsis* may be translated as *making* or *manipulating*. We may observe some system characteristics as being autopoietic when, for example, organizations continuously reproduce themselves, enabling continual co-evolution with the environment to transform themselves and adapt through drawing knowledge from the external environment, then reabsorbing and reframing this knowledge in order to adapt, grow, or be sustained (Maula, 2000). This can be seen as learning through action (Small, 2009). Our practical and pragmatic stance on learning and research very much drives us toward this form of knowing.

The term *praxis*, used in Table 3-1, has two associated rationalities that give rise to English equivalents. The first is through doing virtuous performance, so praxis is imbued with higher level motives of practice that seek excellence in performance through deliberation and reflection. The second meaning of praxis is associated with dialogue and perception-sharing between novice and expert, in a tacit-to-explicit knowledge-sharing cooperation between individuals or groups that leads to the development of competencies and keener insights. It was only late in the thesis work undertaken by Paul that he realized that for the past 40 years he has been using praxis as his way of knowing and professional development. The Winter et al. (2006) fifth research direction is very much about praxis. An important aspect of our philosophical stance is therefore praxis. As Prilleltensky (2001) observes, praxis refers to the unity of theory and action and involves activity cycles that include philosophical, contextual, need, and pragmatic considerations. Cicmil (2006) sets this in a project management context by saying that:

> The notion of praxis becomes central to theorizing skills, knowledge, and competencies. "Praxis" is a form of action that is fundamentally contingent on context-dependent judgment and situational ethics. (p. 30)

Praxis becomes more than best practice because it also informs reflection. Our work is a result of Paul's research as a reflective practitioner, Derek's reflection as a practitioner and academic, and the reflective feedback provided by a community of practice (CoP) that Paul participates in to test and validate the insights and ideas emerging from our research. CoPs are described by Wenger (Wenger et al., 2002) as "groups of people who share a concern, a set of problems, or a passion about a topic, and who deepen their knowledge and expertise in this area by interacting on an ongoing basis" (p. 4). The CoP that Paul tapped into during the research for his PhD was extensive and valuable because he was continually posing reflections, questions, suggestions, and commentary to its members, who responded with their reflections, ideas, comments, and feedback. This was accomplished through literally thousands of conversations and emails over a three- to four-year period.

Theôria or epistêmê is also associated with dialogue, deduction, and deliberation and can be translated into English as *insight*. Weick (1995b) classifies theory with other synonyms such as guess, proposition, hypothesis, speculation, and supposition. These terms all sound very hazy and imprecise, yet we have been led to believe that theory is something grand, noble, and worthy of respect. This is true to a large extent, but the root of the term "theory" implies uncertainty and tentativeness, as well as the sense of being received from one's observation and therefore being interpreted. A theory is a starting point or an accepted staging post on a journey to discovering a wider view of "truth." Weick is well known for his extensive and authoritative efforts to justify what he calls "sense-making"—i.e., understanding and knowing through making sense of situations using personal experience, access to information, and other forms of knowledge. He refers to sense-making as a process of *bricolage,* which means simply being flexible enough to make use of whatever useful tool comes to hand in performing a task (Weick, 1989; 1995a; 2001b; Weick, Sutcliffe, & Obstfeld, 2005).

3.2.2 Ontological Stance and Operating Paradigm

Sewchurran (2008) cites the philosopher Heidegger's belief that "every science presupposes some conception of the being of the entities that are the objects of its enquiry. This conception is often referred to as ontology" (p. 322).

We all tend to believe that the way we see the world is real and that everyone else sees the world the way we do, but in doing so we forget that a worldview is shaped by a myriad of personal and individual incidents and experiences from which our brains create meaning that is tested through the feedback of experience. Since each of us has a personally and individually wired brain that is continually being rewired through our experiences (Greenfield, 2000; 2001), we naturally have shades of meaning that are shared with others only in an overall sense, rather than being cloned and identical.

Ontology can be seen as our point of view, perspective, or the lens through which we view the world and truths pertaining to the world. In a traditional project management frame (a way of conceptualizing and believing in what we perceive), our worldview could be viewed as our perceptual scope. Our ontological stance in this work is framed, in part, from the point of view of the project management practitioners Paul interviewed for his PhD, who shared their lived experiences with him through the medium of rich pictures that expressed their worldview.

Our ontological stance is also framed from our way of making sense, as reflective practitioners, of those interviewees. It is further influenced by Paul's reflections on his 40 years of project management practice through diaries in which he recorded his thoughts, experiences, and responses. So, we bring to this study a rich source of worldviews and reflective experience.

The term "paradigm" has been used to mean a range of different ways of understanding the world, or an overarching way that truth is perceived and phenomena are made sense of. Morgan (2007) provides no less than four uses for the term: as a worldview, as an epistemological stance, as shared beliefs within a community, and as a model example. Smyth and Morris (2007) argue that the use of the term depends to an extent upon the intended purpose. For example, they draw our attention to prevailing traditional project management paradigms as project management from a systems point of view, from a temporary organization point of view, or from a strategic direction point of view. So, paradigms are a convenient way of generally making sense, with a belief that a certain set of rules and protocols (epistemology) holds true for that approach.

Morgan's (2007) view of "paradigms as shared beliefs within a community of researchers who share a consensus about which questions are most meaningful and which procedures are most appropriate for answering those questions" (p. 53) resonated with us. However, we see our paradigm of project management as being in fact a mixture of "truths." We accept project management as a "planning and control" paradigm, where it can be applied to more traditional and ordered contexts (as discussed in Section 2.7.1 and illustrated in Figure 2-5). We also accept project management as being valid in a context that is highly unordered or even disordered (as are the cases with many aid disaster relief projects). In these types of projects, as we pointed out in Section 2.7.1, the "science of muddling through" and the use of improvisation and other less constraining approaches may also be valid, given that project management delivers a means to establishing and gaining commitment to a project vision and set of milestones and a broad and sustainable set of forward directions.

By embracing an eclectic group of project management paradigms, we see ourselves firmly established in the Morgan (2007) metaphysical pragmatic paradigm research camp. This view does not reject positivism, for example, where it may be useful to explain phenomena and where there is a creditable body of expert opinion to support this approach. Nor does it reject a constructivist view, which assumes that "reality" and "truth" are socially constructed through groups of people agreeing on common labels for what they perceive. This means that we can support the use of "fact-based" data such as cost success being the ability to realize a project within its budget, while also accepting that the meanings of "budget" and "expended cost" are also contestable. Thus, we are released from the dogmatism of blindly sticking with one particular project management paradigm (such as traditional project management from a planning and control perspective) and ignoring an equally useful paradoxical paradigm (such as project management as muddling through or being agile improvisers). We are neither inconsistent nor naïve.

3.2.3 Epistemological Stance

All evidence, insights, and knowledge must be based on a belief of what constitutes valid evidence or proof—i.e., an epistemology. Epistemology concerns itself with the nature of knowledge and truth in terms of justifiable evidence, how that evidence or knowledge is validly acquired, and how we know or are convinced of that level of validity (Oquist, 1978).

We do not wish to get too caught up with big words, which tend to leave most people wondering and wandering. In philosophy, the word "epistemology" is, in theory of knowledge terms, that which is viewed as valid and includes the framework for supporting that validity and how we add to our knowledge and understanding through validity and truthfulness.

We also need to link field data observations back to our literature review to better understand how national and organizational cultures and observable artifacts (such as a bar chart or LogFrame) defined shared values, which had common assumptions at their core. This lies at the heart of epistemology. Readers interested specifically in the role of cultural influence should refer to the work of Hofstede (1991), Trompenaars (Trompenaars, 1993; Trompenaars & Hampden-Turner, 2004; Trompenaars & Prud'homme, 2004) and the GLOBE study (House et al., 2002). What these authorities suggest, broadly, is that "Western" project managers working in a predominantly "Eastern" cultural setting will have great difficulty gaining broad acceptance of the epistemological veracity of a project management paradigm that conflicts with their cultural norms.

Consider the notion of time. The Western notion assumes the primacy of clock or calendar time. Months or weeks on a bar chart have specific meaning in the Western project management planning and control paradigm, as evidenced by lines on the chart representing events and when they should start and end. Eastern concepts of entrained time (Andersen, 2008) may mean to readers of the same chart relationships to crop planting and harvesting seasons or religious festivals. Even within the Christian tradition, Catholic and Protestant Easter and Greek Orthodox Easter occur mostly on different dates. In 2010, as we write this book, one author (Derek) is listening to his Greek next-door neighbors celebrate Easter and, later the same day, will travel to the home of Italian friends to enjoy Easter Sunday dinner with them. Most years, these two celebrations fall on different days. Thus, the nature, validity, and perception of truth, evidence, and facts are culturally embedded. We could extend this cultural lens of epistemology to organizational culture and the differing ways in which accountants and marketers define "true" expenditure. A lot depends on how we code the budgets and expenses.

Raelin (2007) urges us to merge theory and practice to produce better theory, better practice, and better learning that will prepare us for the convergence of theory and practice. He argues that good theory is derived from observation, reflection, and analysis of practice, and that through that duality more realistic theory emerges, which better informs practice in a cycle of praxis. He believes that through dwelling in a situation (the lived experience) and empathically reflecting deeply upon it, the kinds of rich insights that emerge provide highly relevant and salient sources of evidence.

3.2.4 Subsection Summary

What we have tried to illustrate from the above is that, far from being mysterious, perplexing, and highly "academic," our philosophical stance is in accord with early philosophy. Our stance is highly practical, pragmatic, and based on making sense from experience, observation, deliberation, and reflection on evidence gathered from practice and empirical data gathered through sharing dialogue with practitioners. It is "radical" in the original sense of the word, which means core, or key, and as close to the center of truth as we perceive it.

3.3 Research Approach Options and Decisions

One's understanding of reality, knowledge, and the ways to realize them are formed in one's philosophy. This also influences our worldviews and how we *plan, do, review,* and *reflect* (referencing the Kolb [1984] action learning steps) upon this reality and knowledge and the ways to realize and validate them.

3.3.1 Positivist Approaches

The prime governing factor driving any research is the researcher's operating paradigm. Ours has been firmly established as unashamedly pragmatic. This allows us to accept, for example, Paul's 40 years of diaries that log his experiences, observations, and results of projects in terms of positivist measures such as cost control success, time control success, and meeting quality measures established from specifications. We feel able to use these data as valid evidence in framing what we perceive could mean project management success, and we can also use these data as a basis for understanding project management best practice. We can also accept (with certain reservations about their generalizability) the results of studies that used a positivist stance on gathering and analyzing survey data from project managers, which we discussed in our Section 2.3 literature review. On that basis, we also accept the many surveys Paul has undertaken over many decades of projects, which his professional project management practice has delivered for his clients.

3.3.2 Interpretist Approaches

An alternative or complement to the positivist measurement method of gathering data and analyzing it to meaningfully understand phenomena is to work from the group up. This is done using an approach that gathers qualitative data such as observation, opinions, open or semi-structured interviews, or vignette information from chance encounters or informal communication such as email exchanges.

Case studies can be a focal point for such data gathering, while the unit of analysis could be a project, an organizational unit, a person, a team of people, or a situation. We also feel totally comfortable using other qualitative research approaches such as soft systems methodology (SSM) to explore the messiness of the lived experience of project managers. This was one of the key approaches that we used, and in the next chapter we will explain how we used SSM. Our purpose in using this approach was to find a way to understand the lived experience of aid project management team members. SSM has been effectively used in several project management contexts (Maqsood, Finegan & Walker, 2003; Winter & Checkland, 2003; Maqsood, 2006; Winter, 2009), as well as in aid project contexts. A thesis by Crawford (2004b) on the effectiveness of project monitoring and evaluation in the aid world, for example, gives a deeper treatment of aid development project management. It also assimilates the work of Checkland and others into aid project M&E through the application of SSM conceptual modeling techniques. Rose (1997) argues that SSM may be a problem-structuring tool, a good-fit research tool, a triangulation tool, and a theory-testing and generation tool.

When reviewing the development and evolution of SSM over a thirty-year span, Checkland (2000), the originator of SSM, finally placed emphasis on three key context questions related to what he calls the "root definition" of models for solution. These questions are: *What* to do (P), *How* to do it (Q), and *Why* do it (R)? Similar questions are applied through different forms of action research (Checkland & Winter, 2006).

The basic SSM approach uses a seven-step process, as illustrated in Figure 3-1 below.

A "messy" problem is identified in its unstructured form as a wicked problem, where there is no one correct answer and the question is difficult to define. The problem is expressed by a series of "rich pictures," which are cartoon-like representations of issues, emotions, and general perceptions of what is going on in all its messiness. Rich pictures are gathered through a process of dialogue and mutual exploration between the researcher and respondents who are embedded in the lived experienced of the situation. These rich pictures are very powerful because they not only collect and represent data about tangible artifacts, but also present emotions and feelings. The next process moves from the "real world" or lived experience to a system-thinking conceptualization of what may be going on. This leads to the explication of the situation as a (soft) system through what is called a root definition that links the situation to a host of subsystems and systems, along with some recommendations about how to address the identified messy problem. The next phase moves from the conceptual systems world back into the "real world," where a harsh

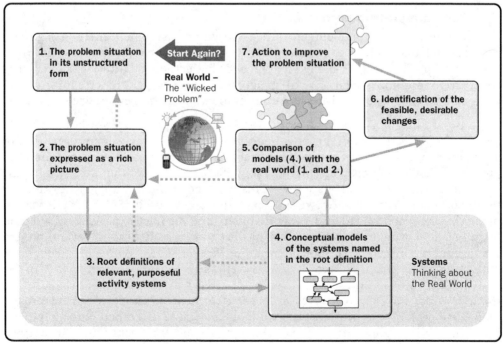

Figure 3-1   Soft Systems Methodology Seven-Step Process: Source, adapted from Checkland (1999)

reality check is made against the conceptual models. This allows a series of feasible actions to be determined, along with a prioritization of what practical measures can be adopted, when, and how. Action then follows, and the cycle may be repeated as many times as are necessary and feasible.

What was most valuable in Paul Steinfort's PhD research was the realization that the SSM approach for steps one to three (see Figure 3-1) revealed a rich stream of tacit knowledge about the "lived experience" of these case study participants which we had never expected to gain access to. Paul performed the SSM rich picture exercises on site visits to Aceh in Indonesia and, as a consequence of being at the case study project sites, he had to experience the discomfort and danger of being in a war zone as well as exposing himself to health hazards in the post-tsunami reconstruction effort. This meant that the people he worked with to develop the rich pictures (a process that will be discussed in more depth in Chapter 4) were able to provide him with deep, explicit, factual, as well as tacit emotional data. Also, because Paul was for that time embedded within the context of the studies' messy situations, he was able to gain an internalized, empathic appreciation of the situation. While it must be acknowledged that this can also impose bias on the data gathering and analysis steps in the SSM process, the pragmatic paradigm adopted by Paul meant that such potential biases were recognized and guarded against as much as practicable. Further, the expectation and the epistemological stance taken supported taking an evidence-based view, as well as triangulation, via extensive validation of meaning through the evolution of the rich pictures.

It is also worth noting that the feedback Paul received from respondents through this process of developing rich pictures, coupled with the observations received through feedback from his CoP, provided an unprecedented opportunity for reflection by respondents and the CoP members in the true manner recommended by Raelin (2007). This approach indicated that SSM tools such as the development of rich pictures, the use of the conceptual model, and the subsequent testing of that model in the lived world demonstrate a high level of evidence for praxis as opposed to limited reflection on practice.

3.3.3 A Pragmatic Action Learning Approach

In Section 3.1.2 above and in Table 3-1, the term *praxis* was presented as a form of reflective action. A further option available through using qualitative research methods and sense-making research approaches is that action science and action learning can be deployed to deal with the kind of research questions we were trying to address.

To understand what the antecedents of project management best practices may be, and in particular how the aid project world may provide valuable lessons to the traditional project management world, we decided to test the lessons learned through an action learning approach. We used Paul's CoP as a vehicle for active reflection on what was being unearthed by the research over the three years of its duration. This was done via email exchanges and then a full-day workshop where findings were presented from the SSM and background literature review and background reflection on Paul's 40 years of project management practice. This workshop served as a quasi-experiment in a typical action research manner. Notes and responses were gathered and analyzed.

A further action learning cycle was triggered as a result of a natural disaster in February 2009, in our home state of Victoria, Australia, in which a devastating bushfire wreaked havoc on numerous communities and destroyed whole townships. Paul was invited by the Bushfire Recovery and Reconstruction Authority[2] to contribute project management advice to the state government, and not only were approaches emerging from the findings of the research studies considered, but they were then executed and tested in real time and in a real, live setting.

In respect of knowledge to be gained or lessons to be learned, we needed a methodology that would not only work robustly and with minimal complexity, but also enable a process to be both understood and formed through different environments and contexts. Action research can address this dilemma in general, but a depth of support may still be needed in philosophical and project practice in the theories of knowledge and the understanding we may draw from them. This shaped our focus on the relevant epistemologies to work within and with action research. Dick (2009) argues that action research subsumes a range of other research approaches, such as action learning, appreciative inquiry, and SSM.

Action learning and action research follow a plan>act and observe> reflect cycle (McNiff & Whitehead, 2000; Dick, 2002b; Zuber-Skerritt, 2002) that is based upon Kolb's (1984) classical experiential learning cycle of concrete experience, reflective observation, abstract conceptualization, then active experimentation. What struck Paul was how similar this was to what he has been doing in his practice for 40 years, and it was also seen as similar to the project management cycle by Hughes, Ndonko, Ouedraogo, Ngum, and Popp (2004). They saw the action learning initiation thematic concerns as being similar to situational analysis in a project management setting: the plan phase of action learning is similar to objectives setting; the briefing process equates to action planning; the act and observe phase of action learning is similar to implementation of a project and its monitoring; and, finally, the reflect phase of action learning matches the evaluation of project outputs and their impact as outcomes.

Further, a pragmatic approach to action research can be usefully deployed as a validation tool. As Oquist (1978) suggests:

> Action research is scientific research within the pragmatic position. It corresponds to the pragmatist view of how man produces and justifies knowledge and is backed by the pragmatist positions with regard to the union of theory and practice and the place of values and ideology in the process of the production of knowledge. Indeed, the pragmatist position maintains that only action research as operationally defined in this essay can truly produce scientific knowledge. (p. 154)

According to Shalin (1992)—in a very interesting philosophical paper that many readers would find of value in understanding the foundations of pragmatism—pragmatism is closely linked to, and supported by, critical theory. He cites Immanuel Kant's exhortation to question assumptions, and his contention that "reason could no longer derive its mandate from divine inspiration or natural law but must lay its own standards for judging the true, the good, and the beautiful" (p. 239), as well as

---

[2]See URL http://www.wewillrebuild.vic.gov.au/ for a report on the first 12 months of activity.

Karl Marx's appeal for "a ruthless criticism of everything existing" (p. 240). He also echoes George Mead with respect to a discussion of the roles of reason and value:

> From a central preoccupation with the mastery over things, reason now turns toward the questions of value. To use Weberian terminology, reason becomes substantive; that is, it reevaluates values, rationally resolves social conflicts, and endeavors to revamp the entire social order from which it sprang. (p. 248)

This discourse may sound, to many project management practitioners and researchers who hold a positivist worldview, somehow rarefied and out of touch with reality, but in our view the discourse lies at the core of reality. Drawing on concepts of value and values is imperative to allow us to consider cross-cultural issues (national or organizational subcultures as discussed in Section 2.7.2) in interpreting rich pictures and in making sense of action learning research results. Value is what counts to an individual. Indeed, the value proposition (Anderson, Narus, & van Rossum, 2006) is a powerful management tool for delivering what appeals to an individual. As we saw in Section 2.7.2, values lie at the core of culture and, therefore, at the core of understanding (which is a core part of Paul's PhD thesis). This leads to the notion of reason lying at the heart of validation or perceived "truth." However, reasoning is more than a purely cognitive activity. Reasoning takes in all our senses and includes highly tacit feelings such as empathy and sympathy. These senses, as we noted in relation to emotional intelligence quotient (EQ) (see Section 2.7.3), are vital to our appreciation of situations and, therefore, to our consideration of what lies at the core of action learning. Shalin (1992) also states, "Reasonableness is minding embedded in practical activity and embodied in emotionally charged situations" (p. 246). That is, reason is embedded in caring and empathizing, so it links in well with EQ. This further links to notions of what is valid, which is an essential element of reflecting in an action learning cycle.

Within a pragmatic epistemology, validation means being satisfied that results are workable, understandable, and useful. A pragmatic approach to validity, especially in an action science/learning sense, is for us liberating. As Shalin (1992) puts it:

> The pragmatist logic is the logic in use; it stipulates that reality does not always lend itself squarely to yes/no judgments and allows practical knowers to say "perhaps," "it depends," "who knows," and to use other indeterminate truth values that help us handle situational indeterminacy. (p. 260)

and

> The quest for pragmatic certainty sensitizes the knower to fuzzy things, multiple realities, semichaotic systems, and it favors participant-observation as a practical way to fathom objective uncertainty. The radically pragmatic epistemological stance also entails clear ethical and political implications: it counsels tolerance to ambiguity, calls for personal responsibility, and encourages rationally motivated dissent. (p. 261)

Oquist (1978) further illuminates how pragmatism is of value as a validation tool, when he states:

> Action or practice in turn must be guided by ideas or theory or they are meaningless. Pragmatism rejects speculative ideas, i.e., theory incapable of guiding action, as unscientific in that they are incapable of justification. (p. 161)

While we can see the benefit of the pragmatist's conceptual frame of knowledge and understanding, we also see that with the extensive knowledge capture of the project management bodies of knowledge (PMBOKs) and the PM&E/Log-Frame knowledge bases discussed earlier in Chapter 2, we need to address the pragmatic paradigm in a critical and improving frame of reference. Further justification of the pragmatic approach can be summarized as follows, using Oquist's argument (1978):

1. Values guide action, and there can be no knowledge without action.
2. Value is the purposeful element in human behavior. Science is a purposive activity, and thus values are part and parcel of scientific research.
3. Practice is policy and action in the context of determinate structures and processes, both those being acted upon and those that condition the outcomes of actions.
4. The relationship between theory and practice within pragmatism is produced by experimental practice.
5. Pragmatism views knowledge as eventual, as an outcome of a given set of operations rather than as something in sufficient existence before the act of knowing (Dewey, 1929).
6. Pragmatism implies that problems, values, ideas, action, and the results of action may be conceptualized at the collective or at the individual level.
7. Indeed, in pragmatism any mode of explanation is considered equally valid, provided that it produces the desired consequences—i.e., it can, therefore, contain multi- or mixed methods, which sit alongside action research.

The other key part of our challenge in this research, and our justification of its validity, was that of the knowledge and theory of "practice." In a paper on the epistemology of practice, Raelin (2007) states that:

> [E]pistemology of practice seeks to explore the tacit processes invoked personally by practitioners as they work through the problems of daily practice. ... Ultimately, a practice epistemology should be able to target learning outcomes that are specifically practice-based, in other words, that derive from learning within the practice. (p. 499)

This process works effectively in a project management context in the same way as the pragmatic action research process does—by the targeting of outcomes and learning from practice (Cicmil, 2006).

3.3.4 Research Methodology

At its core, action research, as outlined previously, comprises a repetition of steps through the cycle of reflect, plan, do, and review. The context and assumptions of the research are defined, and then within that scope, so to speak, the research is refined and worked to resolve outcomes and gain significant knowledge through the extent of the process.

Action research has been seen as meta-research (Dick, 2002a). In this conception of action research, action and research are treated as indissolubly linked. Its spiral is well-equipped for this dual purpose, allowing it to address outcomes of *both action and research, as well as addressing learning at the same time.*

This represents a spiral of iteration between action and critical reflection—a review of what has been learned and then a consideration of how to apply this learning to the next step. From the critical reflection of action research comes an understanding arising from, and leading to, further action. A participatory spiral of alternating action and reflection enables action research to pursue informed action and relevant theory in the service of community and organization development.

Action research has acceptance as a meta-methodology and is seen as having three possible modes in philosophy dating back to Aristotle: "technical" or "making" action (poiesis) (Carr, 2006), which involves participants in working toward hard or physical outcomes; "practical," which is based upon the moral and practical judgment (phronesis) of participants in seeking or "doing" action (praxis); and, finally, "emancipator," which is seen as true "praxis" and, in that light, "critical." However, this third dimension needs to be used carefully in cultures or communities where emancipation or criticism conflicts with prevailing values or mores.

Praxis is not just reflection upon action in itself, but also involves a commitment to human well-being and the search for truth. Praxis requires that those people working through action to outcomes

> make a wise and prudent practical judgement about how to act in this situation. (Carr & Kemmis, 1986, p. 5)

The value of engaging in praxis, as distinct from poiesis or technical action, is brought out very well in community practice research (Prilleltensky, 2001; Prilleltensky & Totikidis, 2006). In research showing the effectiveness of enabling praxis in community-driven programs (Prilleltensky & Totikidis), what came through to us was that once this is understood in a project sense, considerably less external driving is required, and hence less detailed and technical project planning is required. This is very relevant to community outcomes, research, and practice.

Thus, action research, when also understanding and engaging praxis, can more simply and effectively focus on the situation and the potentially wise and prudent actions to achieve outcomes of value. Management action cycles are intertwined with research cycles through critical reflection on both what was learned from the action and what was learned about the research *approach* used and how it may be modified in a subsequent cycle. As previously outlined, a range of cycles is applied in action research. They are typically four-stage cycles and work in a wide range of environments and under differing philosophies and cultures. Hughes et al. (2004) illustrate such models of action intertwined with research. The important link between the management action cycle and the research cycle between each iteration and the next is the addition of deep situational analysis, reflecting upon the lessons learned and the changing context.

As noted earlier, these notions date back to Aristotle and his theory of praxis and are also threaded through both western and eastern philosophies. Within the last century, the action research cycle is also reflected in quality management (the PDSA—Plan/Do/Study/Act cycle) and is probably best summarized, as previously outlined (Reflect/Plan/Do/Review or Reflect/Plan/Act/Observe) (Kemmis

& McTaggart, 1988). This cycle can be applied over different timelines or in connected, but different, timelines within a broader situation. This enables the modeling of the cycles and the research and related projects, conceptually, as cycles within, or working in alignment with, other cycles. Situational analysis occurs at the moment at which the two cycles of action and research are the same, and mediates between previous action and future potential.

This realization has been reflected by modeling of project-/research-related work in both project management and action research (Attwater, 1999; Zuber-Skeritt & Perry, 2002; Hughes et al., 2004).

A good framework within which these cycles can be worked is outlined by Argyris and Schön in their "Theory in Action" (1974). The theory has three components:

1. the *situation* in which the action is taking place
2. the *outcomes*, which it is intended to achieve
3. the *actions*, which are expected to achieve these outcomes

This is captured quite effectively by Dick (2002a; Dick, Stringer & Huxham, 2009) in his assertion that action-to-outcomes occurs with the surrounding situation, which must be critically analyzed within that context.

Single-loop learning is gained from the ongoing reviews of the action cycles, and double-loop learning from the less often but more telling reflections and evaluations of outcomes within the context situation. By understanding and bringing praxis to bear, as outlined previously, wise outcomes or prudent action can also be enacted, evaluated, and possibly validated within this relatively simple and workable situation analysis of prudence and wisdom in action.

Also, and in reference to Gharajedaghi's (2006) two key concepts in this research, if one is able to detect a mismatch in planned and actual actions or outcomes (diagnosis), and then able to plan and do actions, which avoid that mismatch in the future (prescription), then one has truly learned. This is very relevant to all project evaluation work, and to this research in particular, in that through our methodology, models, and practice we constantly review or **monitor** actions (diagnosis) and the planned versus actual mismatches that inevitably occur, and then we reflect upon or **evaluate** the future outcomes (prescription) (Crawford, 2004a). This is a fundamental process, which has been embedded in project and program management over many decades now. In other words, we can all learn from our mistakes, and some learn markedly better than others. The better the methodology for reviewing and reflecting, monitoring and evaluating, diagnosis and prescription, single- and double-loop learning, and authentic leadership, the better the learning and understanding. We will monitor and evaluate our learning and understanding through each cycle.

This will also be reviewed in light of the hierarchy of "information," "knowledge," and "understanding" previously referred to (Gharajedaghi & Ackoff, 1984; Gharajedaghi, 2006; 2007). The knowledge gained can be either single- or double-loop learning, as previously stated. The capture and validation of knowledge demand the best treatment here, too. This dual or double-loop learning loop aspect of action research (AR) is illustrated in Figure 3-2.

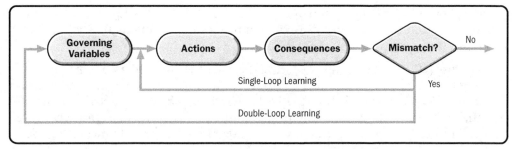

Figure 3-2   Double-Loop and Single-Loop Learning: Source, adapted from Argyris and Schön (1996).

This can be expanded upon within the overall methodology that we may adopt in this research, provided we take in summary terms the analysis of the situation (where the action is planned or taking place, its intended outcomes and the actions that are expected to achieve those outcomes, the flow chart/cycle outlined in Figure 3-2). This can reveal the situation analysis leading to the planned outcomes and the action required to achieve them. Single-loop learning occurs when we implement actions and monitor/review the consequences of those actions. Double-loop learning (i.e., research) occurs when we evaluate the outcomes of those actions and hence reflect upon the governing variables for those outcomes and the significance of the learning emanating from the whole process.

Therefore, our cycle process and key interaction/situation analysis is as shown below.

The action research has two levels:

1. The evaluation of the outcomes in critical and pragmatic review
2. The ongoing review of action to produce value and resolution of the project action

The analysis of the situation, or of the environment and the context, is then resolved through different modes for different stages.

> Situation analysis is repeated in each cycle because the situation changes as an outcome of the action that is implemented and because of other forces in the system and its environment. (Hughes et al., 2004, p. 9)

In this thesis, **research Cycle 1** is through **literature review and reflective practice. Research Cycle 2** is through **SSM within a reflective practice action research** paradigm. **Research Cycle 3** is, again, through a **reflective practice action research** methodology, applying the significantly improved model of Cycle 2 and applying new methodological and contextual situation analysis understandings.

> Sometimes the first cycle is an exploration of the situation (a reconnaissance); the second is an attempt to improve or change (an intervention), and the third is an evaluation of the intervention. (Melrose, 2001, p. 166)

We have taken the first cycle as an exploration of the situation—derived from the literature, present practices, and epistemology. The second cycle comprises the intervention and the validation of the practice and practitioner peer's use of that practice, both in that context and outside of it. Finally, we have taken this work to a different environment and groups to further test, evaluate, and realize better theory and understanding.

Melrose (2001) underscores repeating the cycles within AR as important and as needing to be both "realistic" and "regular" (p. 166). These terms are synonyms for "rigorous" (Roget, Roget, & Roget, 1980). Melrose's definition captures some, but not all, of the rigor of our methodology. We take this rigor to an even higher level, because in our critical reflection we also integrate each key planned outcome as part of the cyclical evaluation.

> The use of critical reflection in each cycle allows the action (or change, or improvement, or intervention) to be integrated with research (or building understanding about the process and the practice or evaluating progress or generating theory). (Melrose, 2001, p. 166)

So, how do we evaluate each outcome, using what criteria, and to what degree of rigor? If we take standard evaluation theory (Reeler, 2007; Smith, 1996, 2001, 2007; Lau, 1999; Zuber-Skerritt, 2002; Fishman & Neigher, 2003; Crawford, 2004a; Hughes et al., 2004; Stame, 2004; Larsen & Cottrell, 2006; Blamey & Mackenzie, 2007; Pollack, 2007; Bourne, 2008; Doty, 2008; Khang & Moe, 2008; Melles, 2008; Crist, Parsons, Warner-Robbins, & Mullins, 2009; Ika et al., 2009; Melles, 2009), we can have a planned outcome, reflect upon what impact the actual outcome had on the overall objective, and reflect on our understanding of the difference.

Presumably, we do have a progressive growth in understanding, but each cycle will bring keys, greater or lesser, in themselves. This enables both a comparative and an overall summation of the impact and validity of the research. Then, we can achieve triangulation in more than one form, the first being edits achieved through rigorous peer reviews in outcomes and practice and the rigorous action research methodology already outlined and then in place.

3.3.5 Validation of Action Learning Outcomes

So, how can a pragmatic action learning approach be seen as valid?

- First, the discussion in Section 3.3.3 continually reinforces the idea that, to be valid, action learning results and recommendations for action must be workable and practical. The proof is assessed through how practical they are (Johansson & Lindhult, 2008).
- Second, recommendations and actions should make sense and the purpose and results should be understandable, rather than emerging from some kind of "black box" outcome. Senge (1990; Senge, Kleiner, Roberts, Roth, & Smith, 1999) sets out a workable process for making sense of evaluating knowledge or value. It first relates to the objective or goals, which are defined by the outcomes that will enable the objective and the actions that will deliver those outcomes. He points out that the most effective measures are most likely to be relative ones, hence the need to include the "soft" as well as the "hard" measures.
- Third, the resulting action should be externally valid (that is, able to be applied and tested in other apparently similar contexts) and internally valid (the method and approach being clear and transparent, thus being seen as fair and reasonable, credible, and therefore plausible) (Hope & Waterman, 2003).

- Fourth, to be valid it must make an objective impact (by triggering changes in practice based upon findings). This is supported by the whole pragmatic epistemological and philosophical framework discussed in Section 3.3.3.

A related validation question arises: If the proposed approach is valid, then what are the parallels between action research and project management or evaluation that make this study relevant to the project management community?

A recent observation by Sankaran, Tay, and Orr (2009) helps to answer that question. They say:

> If you consider how experienced project managers solve "unusual" problems that arise in their projects, you will notice similarities with the processes used in the research projects discussed. Project Managers often make sense of the problem situation through a combination of hard facts, observations and "selective" communication with stakeholders before they come up with a workable situation. Often, the solution is implemented using a plan-do-check-act process that resembles an action research cycle. (p. 120)

Paul designed an innovative method of evaluating each action learning cycle that met these four validity criteria and addressed the justification of taking a pragmatic approach to action learning and outcome validity. Validity criteria are categorized as being workable, making sense, being externally and internally valid, and making an objective impact. From an action learning cycle perspective, each iteration in the cycle should have a cumulative impact. This means that understanding is enhanced in each reflection part of the cycle and informs the next action part until there is sufficient understanding to render further action practically redundant. Once this point is reached, the effort expended in further cycles yields inadequate further value and it is not worth continuing because a point of saturation occurs.

We believe that this makes a significant contribution because it not only further validates action and a pragmatic approach to action learning, but it also provides a useful validation model that can be applied to any reflective learning exercise by a practitioner or organization. Additionally, this validation approach can be used to determine when the action learning cycles approach saturation because all four measures of the validation criteria should converge as being rated "high" when saturation is close or has been reached.

So, how do we evaluate each outcome, using what criteria, and to what degree of rigor? If we take standard evaluation theory (Crawford, 2004b; Stame, 2004; Pollack, 2007; Khang & Moe, 2008; Ika et al., 2009), we can have a planned outcome, reflect on the impact the actual outcome had on the overall objective, and hence reflect on our understanding of the difference. But what criteria should we use?

Again, we do have a progressive growth in understanding, but each cycle in itself will bring keys to increased understanding, to a greater or lesser degree. This enables both a comparative and an overall summation of the impact and validity of the research. Then we can achieve triangulation in more than one form. The first form of triangulation is achieved through rigorous peer review in outcomes and practice and the rigorous action research methodology already outlined and then in place.

This helps us understand how the community of peers is chosen to assess what is workable and practical in a project management context. More rigor can be added by enabling the key validity testing from a critical pragmatist paradigm—sense-making, workability, and communities in practice—and then have it tested through internal and external validation (Weick, 1988; Shalin, 1992; Kvale, 1995; Hope & Waterman, 2003; Larsen & Cottrell, 2006; Johansson & Lindhult, 2008). So, for each outcome cycle we can also evaluate workability and the sense-making effect on the communities in practice.

To enable evaluation of workability, we must first see understanding, in the context of this research objective, as tantamount to sense-making. The simple issue here is whether people or organizations could make sense of the outcomes and confirm understanding sufficiently to make sense of the process or actions in practice. So, we will evaluate or validate understanding in the context of making sense of actions in practice. The next test is that of workability. Does it work in practice when applied in context? The test of workability is a test of outcome in practical terms. Were the outcomes achieved in a technical and practical sense? In some circles, that is referred to as evidence-based evaluation.

This means we may have three tests of outcomes:

1. technical, i.e., was the technical product achieved in the field? (poiesis)
2. practical, i.e., was the practical outcome achieved through purpose and process? (praxis)
3. community in practice, i.e., was the community satisfied with the result or impact?

This approach provides a robust form of effective triangulation additional to the rigor of ongoing cycles and the dialectical developmental improvement that comes from that triangulation and critical reflection.

Our key criteria for outcome evaluation of this research, as outlined above, are:

• understanding by the practitioner or practice participants, i.e., sense-making
• the extent to which outcomes could be put to work in practice, i.e., workability
• the extent to which these outcomes could be taken in different contexts or environments (internal and external validation)
• the extent to which the above, in each research cycle outcome, impacted on the overall objective of the research project

This enables highly focused action research and project evaluation triangulation acting as dialectical devices not offered through other methods of research (Eden & Huxham, 2006), which may then, together, powerfully enable the best understanding and practice.

3.4 Chapter Summary

The purpose of this chapter was to provide an outline, albeit in some depth, of various ways in which the research question could have been addressed. The purpose of the kind of research we undertook (addressing pragmatic practitioner-oriented problems) was to better understand a project management practice situation or problem so that we could recommend action that could be taken to remedy that problematic situation.

We therefore began the chapter with a consideration of philosophy, ontology, and epistemology so that we could frame our research in a context, which enabled readers to understand where we stood on issues of what we believe is valuable about this research and what we consider to be the valid truth and understanding that flows from the research. This informed the readers' view of how valid, and therefore useful, the work might be. That section was split into logically sequential subsections. The first one addressed our philosophical stance, and in doing this we explained terms and ideas that might be new to many readers and therefore worth clarifying and explaining. The second subsection discussed our ontological and operating paradigm so that readers could understand what perspectives we were taking on the research question. The third subsection discussed our epistemological stance, what we considered to be valid evidence to use, and how to validly use that evidence to draw conclusions. We then summarized that section, classifying our worldview and approach as pragmatic and practically consistent with our own experiences and professional journeys in the project management world.

We continued with a discussion on research approach options. We talked about positivist and interpretivist approaches to research, the latter including a discussion of SSM as a methodology for sense-making as well as problem-solving. We then discussed action learning as another possible and useful research approach and set this in the context of a pragmatic paradigm consistent with our stated philosophical stance.

This naturally led to a subsection devoted to validity, because readers and potential critics of this work are entitled to know how we justified our research approach and why we believe it is credible. Throughout this subsection, we foreshadowed how we would justify the discussion in the following chapter on how the research was actually done.

In summary, then, this chapter was about defining terms, underpinning understanding on research stance and approach options available for us and outlining the rationale for making our choices.

4

Research Undertaken

4.1 Chapter Introduction

The purpose of this chapter is to present an account of how the research from Paul Steinfort's PhD actually unfolded and how it supports the research question addressed by this book.

The chapter is structured in six sections and details three sets of action learning phases through which the research was undertaken. The first two sections provide a more detailed explanation of how the action learning approach, as discussed in Chapter 3, was taken forward. The following three sections provide details of action learning cycles 1, 2, and 3, and the chapter concludes with Section 6 as a chapter summary.

4.2 The Adopted Research Approach in Detail

Expected research outcomes have the objectives of:

1. summarizing project management success/best practices and their antecedents in general practice
2. realizing and validating a significantly improved methodology for the antecedents/necessary front-end program/project monitoring and evaluation through grasping lessons learned from aid/relief projects
3. providing action research and project management process improvement so that people close to a project can bridge identified gaps in project management practice including, but not limited to, aid/relief projects

The key methodology was one of action research, whereby the ongoing process of both action and research was enabled by the Kolb (1984) four-stage cycle of *evaluation, planning, action*, and *reviewing* in both the regular problem-solving or project cycles and the more significant research cycles where double-loop progressive learning is evaluated and validated. Derek fulfilled the role of facilitator in this practical, action-learning, PhD thesis approach and acted as catalyst, mentor, advisor, and co-creator of knowledge through a cooperative consultancy process to help Paul and his CoP transform their understanding of the antecedents of project management best practice. The thesis research and core action research efforts became a sound and rigorous collaborative effort, as advocated for this type of research by Zuber-Skerritt and Perry (2002).

Therefore, our cycle process and key interaction/situation analysis was as shown below, with the action research comprising two levels:

1. the evaluation of the outcomes in critical and pragmatic review
2. the ongoing review of action to produce value and resolution to the project action

The situation analysis, or the analysis of the environment and the context, was then resolved through different modes for different stages. This is important because

> the situation changes as an outcome of the action that is implemented and because of other forces in the system and its environment. (Hughes et al., 2004, p. 9)

Research Cycle 1 was undertaken in Paul's PhD thesis through a literature review combined with reflective practice. Research Cycle 2 was undertaken using SSM within a reflective practice, action research frame. Research Cycle 3 was again undertaken through reflective practice action research, applying the significantly improved model of Cycle 2 and the new methodological and contextual situation analysis understandings. As Melrose (2001) observes,

> Sometimes the first cycle is an exploration of the situation (a reconnaissance), the second is an attempt to improve or change (intervention), and the third an evaluation of the intervention. (p. 166)

We have taken the first cycle as an exploration of the situation, emerging from the literature, present practices, and epistemology. We have then taken the second cycle as the intervention and combined with this the validation of the practice and practitioner peers, both in that context and outside of it. Finally, we have taken this work to a different environment and various groups to further test, evaluate, and realize better theory and understanding.

This process, as worked through in Paul's thesis, is shown in Figure 4-1, with the additional understanding of the value of praxis working continuously through the action cycle and the research cycles being reviewed at the conclusion of each outcome.

Figure 4-1 shows Paul's PhD thesis working through classical action research, but with the added value of the lessons of evaluation and the core alignments of project management, project evaluation, and the critical pragmatic epistemologies. This provides a very strong and consistent recycling, evaluation, and validating methodology as well as a rigorous review, critical reflection, and research validation.

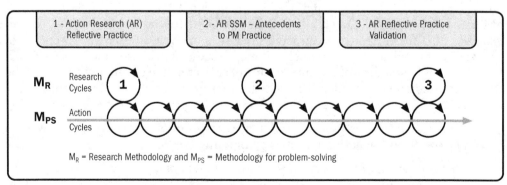

Figure 4-1   Double-Loop and Single-Loop Action Learning Cycle Process

The three research cycles are presented in Table 4-1 below, showing the outcomes as the reflection and action phases of our action research approach.

In Chapter 3, we discussed a number of underpinning research terms, assumptions, and possibilities, and we asserted that Paul had devised an approach that could have wider implications for enhancing people's ability to be reflective practitioners. He used a pragmatic action learning approach that comprised three cycles, forming three case studies.

The first cycle was to investigate and gain knowledge and understanding of the antecedents of project management best practice. This had three key parts: understanding what project management best practice—or, more specifically—effective practice is; understanding how it is defined; and understanding the antecedents to its effective working. This first phase used a literature review, a review of Paul's extensive collection of reflective diaries and logs of projects he had worked on over a period of 40 years, a number of client and other surveys on project practice and project management success over those years, and feedback received through being a judge on many industry excellence award panels. This first phase represents a kind of retrospective and current action learning cycle, with reflection on the past leading to active research

Table 4-1   Research Objectives and Key Research Outcomes and Action Cycles, Source: Steinfort (2010, p. 103)

Thesis Objective	Outcomes (R)	Action (A)
Understand the antecedents to project management practice – Lessons to be learned from aid/relief projects	1. Summarize project management success/ best practice and their antecedents in general practice	1.1 Summary of critical success factors for all range of projects and aid projects in particular
		1.2 Understanding and synthesizing the methods/ core value of each of the project management body of knowledge methods employed around the world
		1.3 Realizing and summarizing the importance of context/front end factors to project success/ project management practice
		1.4 Summary keys and methods to antecedents for project management practice and success/ preliminary validation testing and planning for stage 2
	2. Realize and validate a significantly improved methodology for the antecedents/necessary front end and project management through lessons learned from aid/relief projects	2.1 SSM/rich pictures from post-disaster project management practice in real environment reflect and synthesize key findings from the field
		2.2 Peer review of key findings/validation
		2.3 Summary of findings, antecedents, method draft/validation
	3. Provide project management process improvement so that people close to the project can bridge identified gaps in project management practice, including, but not limited to, aid/relief projects	3.1 Provide workable processes to community of and in practice for implementation
		3.2 Test/validate/update methods/methodology/ AR/project management process improvement through work in communities of and in practice
		3.3 Summarize findings/AR to project management methodology – synthesis, enduring models, synergies and realizations – validate

of the literature. This led to a reflection of findings, which were subsequently tested with Paul's CoP, to evaluate how they, as a reliable sample of project management practitioners, understood the results and how those results might be applied. One of the results of this phase was a growing realization of how traditional project management practices could benefit from the knowledge Paul gained about the adoption of theoretical project management practices in the aid disaster relief project world.

The second cycle involved an empirical field investigation in Indonesia, of the lived experience of a number of people who worked in this project management world in the recovery and reconstruction after the tsunami disaster of Boxing Day 2004. Paul was able to speak to a range of participants in that context, and thereby gained firsthand empirical knowledge of what issues that world faces. This enabled him to take his reflections on the first cycle, re-evaluate how he saw the research question after completing that part of the second action learning cycle, and put his analysis and synthesis of the findings forward to his CoP for validation in terms of the criteria described in Chapter 3, Section 3.3.5. This involved a one-day workshop in which he brought together, in one location, a number of members of his CoP to discuss and explore findings from the second action learning cycle.

The third cycle turned out to be serendipitous, but in a rather macabre way. Originally, Paul had planned to instigate a third action learning cycle based on a form of workshop, a Delphi survey, or other validation approach. However, nature intervened through a horrendous bushfire, considered the worst in the State of Victoria's history. Many lives were tragically lost, large property losses were sustained (including Paul's sister's home), and the state responded by instigating a disaster recovery authority and plan to coordinate the reconstruction and re-establishment of the many communities destroyed by the fires. As the highly respected CEO of a project management practice in Melbourne, Victoria, Paul was asked by senior government officials to advise and help with the project management aspects of that initiative. This provided the ideal opportunity to conduct the third cycle of action learning, which was to test the efficacy and workability of his findings from stage 2.

In Chapter 3, Section 3.3.5, we discussed an evaluation model with which action research cycles could be assessed. These fell into four broad categories which we used to measure the extent to which criteria for each cycle of gaining additional refinement of the end result had moved toward a rigorous end result. These criteria, and how they were measured, are presented in Table 4-2.

4.3 Action Learning Cycle One

Each of these subsections, for each action learning cycle, will follow the plan-act-observe-reflect cycle. Cycle 1 was the initiating cycle. The plan part of this cycle will explain the approach used, the act-observe part provides much of the substance and content of interest to readers, and the reflect part of the cycle provides an evaluation score based upon the criteria set out in Table 4-2.

4.3.1 Action Research Cycle 1—The Plan Process

The first phase of this research was to investigate and gain knowledge and understanding of the antecedents of project management best practice. This had three key parts—what is project management best practice or, more specifically, effective practice; how is it defined; and how do we understand the antecedents to its effective working?

Table 4-2   Criteria for Measuring Saturation

Criterion	Measure and Description of Measure
Knowledge and Understanding/ Sense-making – How much did this action lead to better knowledge, understanding, and sense-making in the CoP?	0 = Minimally effective 1 = General knowledge – basic knowledge but understanding not applied 2 = General understanding – general knowledge and understanding demonstrated 3 = Effective understanding – but no valid sense-making 4 = Effective sense-making – working knowledge with understanding and sense-making 5 = Very effective sense-making – proven understanding and sense-making
Practice and Workability – How much could that action output be effectively applied in practice?	0 = Minimally effective – not applied 1 = Marginally effective – applied but only marginally 2 = Generally effective – generally applied and with general output 3 = Effective – effective application with workable output 4 = Very effective – effective application with very workable output 5 = Highly effective – very effective application with very effective output
Community Internal and External Validity – How much was understood and workable, internally and externally, in the CoP?	0 = Not effective – not understood or applied 1 = Internally effective – understood and applied, but only internally, not externally 2 = Generally effective – understood and applied internally and externally 3 = Effective – understood and applied effective application internally and externally 4 = Very effective – effective application with workable output internally and externally 5 = Highly effective – very effective application with very effective application both internally and externally
Objective Impact – What value did this action/outcome deliver to the overall objective?	0 = No objective impact 1 = Marginal impact – applied and some output, but of limited value 2 = Reasonable impact – applied with some impact on objectives and output value 3 = Impact and value – effective impact on objective delivering impact value 4 = Effective impact and value – effective impact on objective with output valued 5 = Very effective – very effective objective impact and output value delivered

A good starting point for this review was in the main literature on these aspects, which is actually on critical success factors in either project management or, more generally, project success. As outlined in Chapter 2, Section 2.3, these factors have been typically separated into project success, which is most simply defined as the self-reported satisfaction of the key stakeholders, and project management success, which is the achievement of the traditional project management targets (timeliness, cost, quality), and even more so as defined by the *PMBOK® Guide* methods and measures.

This review was then evaluated at two levels: how success is judged (success criteria) and the factors that contribute to the success of projects (success factors). The overall process was to look at the information, data, or knowledge received through each action step and then to reflect upon each research cycle outcome, achieved or not, through the sum of those steps.

These project success factors were developed in light of the literature and other information available and then, in this case, from a forward view of reflective practice. This reflective practice has two general parts—particular reflective practice, and a community of practice.

4.3.2   Action Research Cycle 1—The Act-Observe Process

This literature and other information, together with the reflective practice and process review, formed the framework of ideas for the formative and preparatory stage of this research project. First, though, we needed to look at the situation analysis, defined as the understanding of project management best practice, or, at a minimum, what may be seen as effective practice and its necessary antecedents. The literature was reviewed extensively in Chapter 3 of Paul's thesis, and some of that review is presented in Chapter 2 of this book. However, it was also necessary to provide the background of the reflective practice and related informal action research formalized here because it also provided guidance based upon the adopted epistemology and practice for this research.

This literature review gave background to the understanding and development of summary project success factors and the determination of their two key categories in light of both this and earlier research. This is not to be confused with the research project success criteria, which measure the achievement of objectives judged to be successful by the key stakeholders of the research project, as set out in Table 4-2.

We had not expected that the first outcomes and evaluation would bring closure or strong validation to this research project, as in reality they constitute the summative background for the considerably more formative second research cycle. Crawford, Morris, Thomas, and Winter (2006) note with respect to reflective practitioners that, in a project management context, encouraging reflective practice is desirable so that the problems of how "tacit project management knowledge can be best developed and transferred and how can we leverage the 'greybeards' before we lose them" can be addressed (p. 731).

Paul felt that, as a 60-year-old practitioner, he fit the "greybeard" category ideally, so this phase can be seen to have proven value and relevance because he had the background, wisdom, and experience to effectively reflect on his project management experience and the salience of the relevant literature and he had access to other "greybeards" in his CoP to exchange perceptions about what he was reflecting on. This practice review was based on Paul's reflections and those of his CoP who had been engaged in some of the most demanding projects in Australia and who were judged successful by the key stakeholders to those projects. Some of these projects received state and national project management awards, having been additionally judged successful by project management peers and the industry. Additionally, Paul had also served as president of the Australian Institute of Project Management, on post-graduate and graduate leadership committees for education, in training and mentoring in project management, and as lecturer in those courses and programs. This illustrates the scope and depth of experience on which Paul could draw.

The *act* and *observe* process for this reflective practice, and for these findings in particular, evolved primarily from Paul's reflective journals. Then, working from the literature review of critical success factors and criteria for the projects referred to in the previous paragraph, and from work done prior to starting his PhD thesis, he developed 20 possible success factors for each project, which were cross-checked and tabulated. Those factors were applied or tested toward success on each project or program at that time. All of this was then recorded on a spreadsheet to better detail and analyze each project or program and the relevant factors. Key success factors were extracted from that spreadsheet[3] in a summative

---

[3] Paul's entire thesis can be accessed and downloaded through the URL link http://www.psaproject.com.au/.

form and then reviewed during the early PhD thesis writing process throughout 2008 in light of the literature and other information reviewed. Key categories in the extraction related to themes and terms used, such as "external and internal, project, plan, monitor, and evaluate." This review was iteratively undertaken up to early 2010.

This reflective process is, in essence, the one used by Paul's company for the last 25 years. It is the same as that set out in Chapter 3—i.e., plan, do, review, reflect. His professional practice has enabled the successful completion of many of the most demanding projects in Australasia, all of which were carried out through these simple yet robust project cycles. The methodology for this practice is contained within in-house manuals, with an interesting dual-cycle process. Figure 4-2 is an extract from Paul's project management company (PSA) documentation, showing procedures that have been in use for over 20 years.

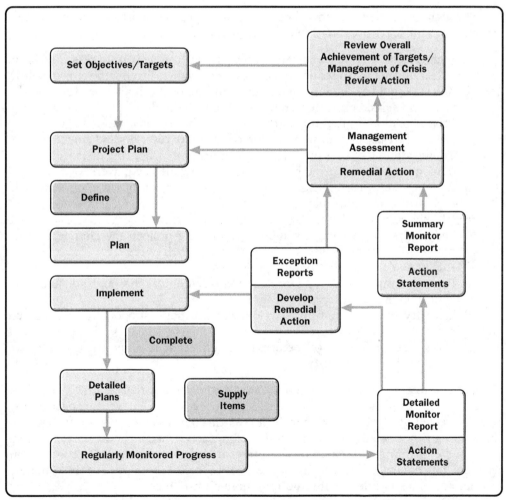

Figure 4-2   Historical Method of Project Cycles for Project Management: Source, PSA

Knowledge was gained and captured through PSA data collection and reporting over 20 years on over 100 projects, with a total value of over AUD$4 billion. This was in addition to insights captured in project management training notes and other materials that formed part of the mentoring and coaching services provided by PSA.

It is worth noting that, as part of the reflective process described above, Paul realized that the traditional *PMBOK® Guide*-type knowledge bases of the time did not fully address the antecedents of project management practice, or, for that matter, stakeholder management and engagement. It is interesting that through recent reflection triggered by this phase in the action learning Cycle 1, the importance of these shortcomings was realized, addressed, resolved, and then used to inform the second action learning cycle.

This research information then needed to be extended beyond the traditional project management base. However, in order to lead into the next action cycle, we first had to realize what was significant in this light, in the history of projects to date.

Through this process, a general but not final summary of project success factors, prior to the antecedent realizations, was identified as follows:

1. A clear mission/vision and agreed on goals, with agreed on success criteria and a clear understanding of desired and expected values driving the project culture
2. Key stakeholder/key resource understanding of the goals/objectives, with a clear and agreed on statement of outcomes defined
3. Project plan and program/method of work being resolved and agreed to by all key parties, including provision of adequate reserves and contingencies
4. The feasibility of that plan (in terms of resources, contingencies, risks, and outcomes) being resolved and signed off on by all key players
5. Adequate resources being committed for the project, based upon details derived from an achievable project plan
6. Clearly stated and understood project management capacity, experience, and staff/senior manager's support, including project governance and dispute resolution procedures to engender trust behaviors
7. Adequate communication and project tools
8. Project competencies and project management skills, and adequate and agreed on organizational structure
9. Integrity, effective communication, commitment, support, team approach, mentoring, and learning
10. (An acknowledgment of) external influences, such as political or cultural awareness and capability

It is interesting, but perhaps not all that surprising, to realize how close these are to the factors presented in Chapter 2, Section 2.3. These Cycle 1 phase results were reviewed by Paul and further discussed through his CoP via an exchange of many (tens if not scores of) emails and in conjunction with the iterative, overlapping, and continuing reference to the literature as part of the PhD process. Paul developed a conceptual model, illustrated in Figure 4-3, that gave monitoring and evaluation, as well as people interaction, more prominence.

This overall summary, supported by the more widely researched practice success factors, was a valuable development leading into the overall research information

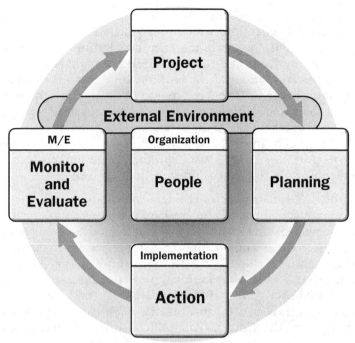

Figure 4-3   Summary Success Factor Model at End of
                  Action Cycle 1

and understanding for stage 2, or the second, possibly most important, research cycle. All of the above was not conclusive in itself, but was quite formative in how it began to frame the key factors into key categories that would get much better communication and resolution as the research progressed to and in the "field."

4.3.3   Action Research Cycle 1—The Reflect Process

In Chapter 3, Section 3.3.4, we presented an evaluation model with which action research cycles could be assessed. These criteria are summarized as follows: knowledge, understanding, and sense-making; workable practice; community internal and external validation; and value to outcome impact. These formed the basis of the review stage of Cycle 1 and were measured on a 0 to 5 scale as outlined in Table 4-3, providing the overall assessment for an action learning Cycle 1.

In this first cycle, we reflected upon how success factors were understood and this knowledge used. This was based on Paul's reflection of how his project management professional practice PSA has operated over the past 20-plus years and how his clients reacted to the way this was retrospectively linked to an action learning Cycle 1.

Table 4-3   Criteria Assessment for Action Learning Research Cycle 1

Knowledge, Understanding, and Sense-Making	Workable Practice	Community Internal and External Validation	Value to Outcome Impact
3	1	1	1
Effective understanding	Marginally effective	Internally effective	Marginal

Paul's current reflections were gained, with the benefit of hindsight, from the action learning Cycle 1 reflection, which took place in earnest during 2008–2009, from having done his PhD research and from concluding many communications via the CoP. Interestingly, his and the CoP's reflections share no significantly different characteristics from those of the vast majority of project management practitioners who were neither sufficiently exposed to or educated in the need to more fully understand the antecedents of project management best practice. He considered himself typical of most project management practitioners of the time—that is, comfortable and confident in the project management frameworks they all worked through. In retrospect, it is so obvious and important for many reasons that these gaps in understanding are realized, addressed, and resolved.

On reflection, the importance of problem-solving to project management and the regular action cycles may be underestimated by academic critics, who may place too much emphasis on project management practices being plan-and-control focused. Problem-solving is vitally important in project management, stakeholder, and project team confidence and as a path to planning, doing, and learning. Without this regular process cycle, no traditional project could actually be successful in practice. This phase of action learning Cycle 1 did not take into account the more recent knowledge and experience gained in the Aceh reconstruction and aid relief program of projects and the Victoria, Australia bushfire reconstruction activities.

The following provides greater detail on the ratings given in Table 4-3:

Knowledge, understanding and sense-making—The first action or deliverable for this is the realization of the range of key success factors for projects and the need for differentiation between project success factors and project management success factors. Further, the factors need to be classified as macro or micro, internal or external, and technical or social. This first activity, however, did bring a newfound understanding of key success factors and also a clearer distinction between project success factors and project success criteria, and the best potential structuring of each of them within an overall research frame. *Rating 3*

Workable practice—In their review of this first action step, Paul and the CoP had gained a much better understanding of the importance of antecedents to project management success in general. It also brought a very workable categorization to the overall frame for research and critical reflection. It helped develop a philosophical and paradigmatic frame for the important second phase research, but mostly it highlighted the fact that traditional project management users, including Paul and others, needed a much better understanding of its necessary antecedents.

It was important to practice, but at the same time it was surprising to realize how much the importance of the antecedents had been underestimated or just not taken into account in traditional project management. Also, it became clear how little the front-end and LogFrame methods, in particular, effectively integrated into project management in practice. *Rating 1*

Community internal and external validation—Several papers were presented at conferences and published through this research work, but it was becoming obvious that there was a gap between the effective practical understanding of, and research into, the interface between antecedents and project management—i.e., it had not been effectively addressed or understood anywhere in the community in general at that time. *Rating 1*

Value to outcome impact—It was of limited value in isolation, but, in time, would prove valuable in support of better understanding overall. *Rating 1*

4.4 Action Learning Cycle Two

Our second action learning cycle, working toward our first outcome, involved all three types of action science methods—technical, practice, and emancipator. The technical position has traditionally and most typically been taken by the *PMBOK® Guide*, the practice by that and other bodies of knowledge which relate to project management practice around the world and the emancipator by the Project Monitoring and Evaluation/LogFrame/Project Cycle Management (PCM) and Theory of Change methods.

4.4.1 Action Research Cycle 2—The Plan Process

Chapter 2, Section 2.4 highlighted the importance of the front end to projects and the way that project success must be seen (as illustrated in Figure 2-2) in context with the impact on the customer (or target for the beneficial change triggered by a project), the success of the business (or organization), and preparing the organization for the future. In Chapter 2, Section 2.5, we also cited the rethinking project management agenda by stating that this research would address all five recommended research themes (Winter et al., 2006). Chapter 2 then continued in Section 2.6 with a discussion and explanation of aid project management approaches and techniques, which are salient to this action learning cycle. The Log-Frame, we contended, is a highly useful project front-end tool, which justifies and clarifies the aims of programs of projects. The monitoring and evaluation (M&E) is part of a results-based management approach that features transparency and accountability (see Figure 2-4) and provides active technical devices that can be used in managing any project. We noted in Chapter 2 that while these tools and devices are widely used in the aid relief project management world, they are seldom considered for use by the traditional project management world, and indeed there is no mention of them in the *PMBOK® Guide* (PMI, 2008a). However, PRINCE 2 (Bentley, 1997; Office of Government Commerce, 2007) does acknowledge these tools and puts greater focus on the front end of projects than is evident from the *PMBOK® Guide*.

Given the apparent gap between practices in the traditional project management world and the aid relief project world, it seemed natural for action learning Cycle 2 to attempt to investigate whether there were possibilities to synthesize the two worldviews and approaches to project management in order to improve project management practices in general. This entailed gaining a better understanding of how project management is perceived by the aid relief project world.

In Chapter 3, Section 3.3.2, we explained the soft systems methodology (SSM) technique and how it may be useful in studying a "messy situation or problem," and through that process enable us to better understand the lived experience of participants. We felt that the conduct of an SSM study would help us understand why the gap between the traditional project management world and the aid relief project world exists and what we may be able to do to bridge that gap.

Paul had been involved in a major aid recovery program of projects in 1974 as part of the recovery from the devastation following Cyclone Tracy, which had struck Darwin, in the Northern Territory of Australia, in December of that year. His role was to manage various projects for the recovery, and, along with his direct experience of working in a post-disaster situation, he also had diaries and professional reflection notes from that period to which he could refer. He had been asked to undertake reviews of the program of projects taking place in Aceh, Indonesia, as part of the post-tsunami recovery effort, and at the same time he was working pro bono for SurfAid, an organization that delivers health aid projects in the outer islands of Indonesia, many of which had also been devastated by the tsunami of December 2004.

All of this meant that Paul already had direct experience in this kind of aid/relief project management work and had access to interview a number of participants in aid recovery and reconstruction projects in post-tsunami programs of projects throughout Indonesia and the region. Our plan was for Paul to undertake a field visit to gather direct data in the form of rich pictures, thereby gaining an in-depth understanding of the lived experience of those involved in aid relief projects in that region. Project Management Institute (PMI) had generously funded a proposal that allowed this to take place, and so we were able to gain valuable data in what became action learning Cycle 2.

This cycle followed a pragmatic paradigm and the aims and epistemological stance were consistent with our pragmatic worldview.

In terms of the research cycle, we wanted to learn more about the lived experience of aid relief project management team members in the field. Paul's direct experience in similar situations enabled him to empathically engage with interviewed participants in the study, while respecting their view of "reality" and not questioning or judging their perceptions of project management practice, what they valued as helpful to them, and what they saw as hindrances.

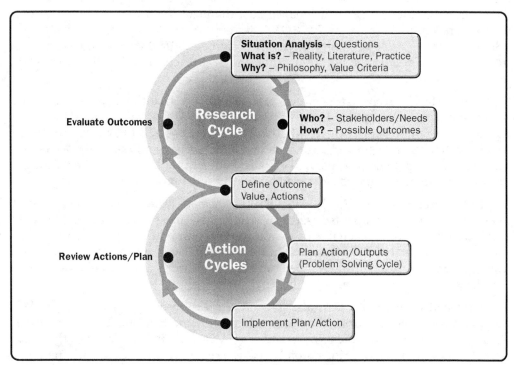

Figure 4-4   Situation Analysis at Start of Action Learning Cycle 2

The advantage of SSM and the kind of data gathered through co-development of rich pictures is that a whole range of otherwise neglected stakeholders are identified and their stories are told. At the same time, the rich pictures help to reveal a range of emotions and feelings that bring to life the who and how of action and help to define outcomes, values, and actions arising out of the projects investigated through SSM, so that the research process can be evaluated.

The action plan in this instance was to determine how to undertake the SSM studies and then actually conduct the field investigation and analyze the resultant data.

4.4.2 Action Research Cycle 2—The Act-Observe Process

The first part of this act-observe cycle for the SSM study was arranging for suitable people to interview and organize the travel arrangements. We originally wanted to gain insights into the aid relief project world through the ontological stance of three levels of management for those types of projects. The first ontological stance was from the perspective of a senior manager responsible for such projects in order to gain insights about what the aims of a program director may be and how they are realized. The second was from that of a project manager practicing in the field. The third was from the perspective of a resident who was engaging in the project as part of a project team, most likely unaware of the project management details of what was going on, but able to view the project from the perspective of a participant with little or no project management experience. We felt that this would provide the necessary triangulation and validity to meet the pragmatic aim for the study to be honest and credible, and potentially provide a useful model that other researchers might in the future follow to investigate similar situations. In all, eight respondents took part, which was more than we first planned for, but we were delighted to gain insights from several people for each ontological stance.

4.4.2.1 SSM–Developing a Rich Picture for Analysis of the Messy Situation

The interviews were mostly carried out onsite in the participants' chosen locations, to best interface with and witness their challenges and problems. This took Paul to the outer reaches of the islands of Indonesia. In each case, the interviewees were very valuable participants, but also appreciated the effort and feedback required in each exercise. The process to enable the development of the rich pictures, which have become such a valuable feature of this research, took considerable time (most of 2008, including the validation and feedback into their accuracy from the participants' points of view), engagement, and effort to complete. This was mainly developed on projects and programs in the post-tsunami and post-earthquake locations of the Indonesian islands near or off Aceh. The interviewees included some of the most experienced and noted players in the post-tsunami and later earthquake recovery, reconstruction, disaster preparedness, and further disaster response around the world.

These participants (or actors, in the SSM context) had substantial responsibilities and experience, and included:

1. A United Nations (UN) consultant with AusAID and Indonesian government training involved in key recovery and reconstruction programs in Nias and Aceh (40 years experience)
2. The Indonesian government high-level responsibility person for recovery and reconstruction in the Aceh and Nias islands (30 years experience)

3. The founder of an international Non-Governmental Organization (NGO) for Recovery and Health Programs on several Indonesian islands (30 years experience)
4. An AusAID-funded Emergency Preparation Program Manager for the Nias and Mentawai islands (15 years experience) with whom Paul worked on tsunami recovery programs
5. A community resident in the area of Lok Nga, Banda Aceh, who lived through the tsunami, lost family members, but then was very involved in the reconstruction and livelihood efforts in his village and has building and construction experience (many years local and international experience)
6. A young field coordinator in the recovery and reconstruction of an American-based NGO involved in both reconstruction and livelihood development in the stricken islands (2 years experience)
7. An Australian-qualified project manager who was working on AusAID and other funded reconstruction projects in Aceh and Yogyakarta and, as an NGO agent and prime contractor, also engaged in program design (12 years experience)
8. The Chief Operations Officer (COO) of an international NGO, working in both Australia and Indonesia after the tsunami and in related health care and Disaster Emergency Preparation and Recovery Programs (7 years experience)

This was a very experienced and well-qualified cross-section of participants from areas of the relevant responsibilities and challenges, so we felt that our plan to represent three ontological stances to enhance the pragmatic validity of this study was justified. It is noted that, in the PhD program initially approved, there was a commitment to develop this action research with only three players (or actors, in the SSM methodology). These numbers were increased in order to be absolutely sure of convergence of opinion about a workable picture of the key steps necessary in gaining the agreed project outcomes.

We could then gain a clearer understanding of the framework for the lessons to be learned from post-disaster aid recovery projects through data gathered via the rich pictures by understanding the antecedents of project management best practice in a range of environments. Or, conversely, we could better understand what seasoned practitioners in these regions and this work see as fundamental to their theory and practice and compare it with the methods available globally. These post-disaster relief projects take place in situations where there is a notable absence of the characteristics of required and identified project management antecedents. We needed to explore and make explicit the often tacitly held assumptions that underpin sound project management practice. In making sense of the data and results from the SSM rich pictures, we also needed to review both best theory and practice (from action learning Cycle 1), to be able to understand the required intellectual infrastructures needed for competent project management practice to be achieved. We did this by comparing project management best practices (as experienced and codified in the literature, and evidenced and demonstrated in practice on widely accepted, successfully completed projects) with project management practice on distressed and troubled projects. Action research through SSM provided us with the clearest way to do this.

A very strong alignment evolved in the key processes that emerged from the eight rich pictures. We used a key color-coded, three-level layering process that

Paul devised and introduced to the SSM process as a valuable development tool to understand and communicate what was thematically going on in this messy project situation (illustrated by colored, labeled ellipses) and how it related to traditional project management processes (indicated by the colors chosen for ellipses and cited quotations). These will be explained later in this subsection.

It is not possible to relate or include all eight rich pictures in the main body of this thesis, but some key examples are shown in order to give the necessary insight into both the very useful process undertaken and the outcomes in a research and development sense. Each picture tells (in excess of) a thousand words, as the old saying goes.

The purpose of this book is not to provide details on the SSM rich picture outputs and the textual interpretation of those stories and their meaning, though much of that is provided in Appendix 5 of Paul's thesis. We aim here instead to summarize key findings as part of the action learning cycle approach. At first glance, the rich pictures may appear overwhelming to the reader. We need to explain how they were co-developed, because the production of such images will be referred to in the next subsection as a reflection on an important research methodology outcome of this work.

A rich picture begins with an empathic dialogue between the researcher and the participant. It takes the same form as any interview. Ethics approval was sought and granted from RMIT University prior to undertaking the interviews. Respondents were fully briefed about the research, its aims and objectives, and how outputs and outcomes would be used.

In the typical interview process, the researcher and respondent need to meet and talk over an extended time period often punctuated by breaks to reflect on the meaning of what was being exposed through the process. The respondent typically recalls an incident or trigger-event for an emotion, concept or important feeling. This is then jointly drawn through iterative sketches, which are then left to "marinate" for a while and are later reviewed for accuracy. Through this iterative and interactive approach, co-learning develops as both partners in the process are forced to challenge assumptions in a genuinely reflective learning process.

Interviews may be taped and a transcript produced, in order to make sense of the data. This can be coded in some way, and various themes often emerge out of the data from which a theory can be generated that helps explain what is going on in the situation under study. This is often referred to as a "grounded theory" approach (Glaser & Strauss, 1967; Strauss & Corbin, 1998; Locke, 2001). The disadvantage of interviews being transcribed and dealt with in this way is that nuances are lost. Sometimes they can be captured if the interview is videotaped rather than just recorded on audiotape, or if the researcher takes notes to record expressions, body language, or other emotional manifestations of the interviewee. However, even these additions do not match the richness and depth of emotive communication that rich pictures potentially hold. Rich pictures are often produced as cartoon-like representations of a series of vignettes, stories, and recalled incidents that together provide a sense of the lived experience being studied. Metaphors such as clouds, bolts of lightning, smiling faces, and other pictorial artifacts are often included. Key snippets of stories may also be used as direct quotations. One of Paul's innovations was the use of colors and overlays to link the rich pictures with theoretical project management constructs such as planning, vision, etc. This will be explained in more depth in the next subsection.

The first rich picture is quite typical of the overall verified outcomes (see Figure 4-5). Full-size A3 rich pictures more clearly illustrate the problems, and sometimes the developed solutions or realizations, of all the key players. This first one was set in a village that was possibly the most publicized and devastated of all. The participant was a resident there when the tsunami struck and remained there during the recovery and reconstruction phases. The interviews for this rich picture were actually carried out overlooking the ocean at a place called Lok Nga, out of Banda Aceh, where the tsunami struck with devastating and extremely destructive force. This person lost members of his family and was heavily involved in community rebuilding after the tsunami.

Readers may note the caption on the upper right-hand side of rich picture 1, Figure 4-5, which depicts an Acehnese saying after the tsunami and the early recovery experience "that Westerners have heart and talk that is bigger than the hand that follows." This relates the Acehnese experience that NGOs such as the UN and other aid agencies were often unable to fulfill the expectations they initially set. This was due to a number of factors, not the least being that they had little or no understanding of the antecedents to project management practice, so that good intentions were

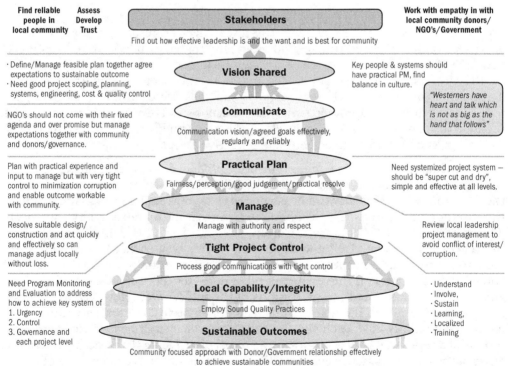

Figure 4-5   Example of a Rich Picture for Action Learning Cycle 2 from a Survivor and Resident of a Village in Lok Nga out of Banda Aceh

not realized. There are many more such captions, depictions, and key realizations evident in this rich picture as in each of the other seven validated ones.

Repeated themes through the rich pictures highlight key points (the importance of the stakeholders, their meaningful engagement, a shared vision of the reconstruction) and the forming of a practical plan which, worked locally and managed toward sustainable outcomes, provides a clear thematic example. This illustrates not only the importance of key stakeholders, but also the need for urgency, flexibility, and practical planning to enable sustainable outcomes. It also touches on the need for trust in working out the key goals for and within the community. It provides a perspective from the ontological stance of an aid recipient and, therefore, "client" stakeholder, as well as from that of the project participant, since all people involved played some role or other in the project realization. This picture helps to highlight expectations as well as lived and felt experience of the impact of the overlaid project management practices that were perceived to have been used in this case study example.

The second rich picture (Figure 4-6) is from the Indonesian government officer responsible for the recovery and reconstruction of Nias and further areas of Aceh, both in the post-tsunami period and after the earthquake that struck three months later. This work in Indonesia took more than three years to manage, following which this person, with his understanding and experience, was seconded to Burma after the devastating cyclones there. He represents another client level, as well as the ontological stance of a high-level administrator of the program of projects.

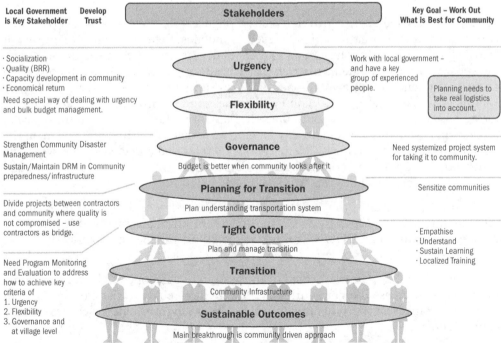

Figure 4-6   Example of a Rich Picture for Action Learning Cycle 2 from an Indonesian Govt. Officer for Nias and Aceh Recovery

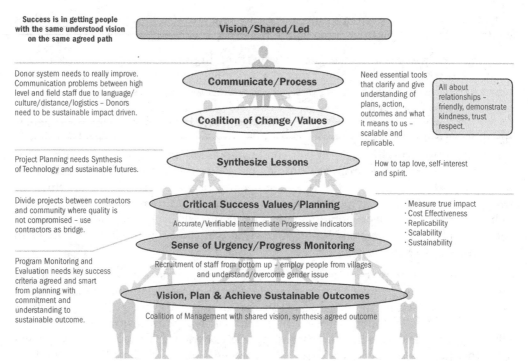

Success is in getting people with the same understood vision on the same agreed path

Vision/Shared/Led

Donor system needs to really improve. Communication problems between high level and field staff due to language/ culture/distance/logistics – Donors need to be sustainable impact driven.

Communicate/Process

Coalition of Change/Values

Need essential tools that clarify and give understanding of plans, action, outcomes and what it means to us – scalable and replicable.

All about relationships – friendly, demonstrate kindness, trust respect.

Project Planning needs Synthesis of Technology and sustainable futures.

Synthesize Lessons

How to tap love, self-interest and spirit.

Divide projects between contractors and community where quality is not compromised – use contractors as bridge.

Critical Success Values/Planning

Accurate/Verifiable Intermediate Progressive Indicators

· Measure true impact
· Cost Effectiveness
· Replicability
· Scalability
· Sustainability

Sense of Urgency/Progress Monitoring

Program Monitoring and Evaluation needs key success criteria agreed and smart from planning with commitment and understanding to sustainable outcome.

Recruitment of staff from bottom up - employ people from villages and understand/overcome gender issue

Vision, Plan & Achieve Sustainable Outcomes

Coalition of Management with shared vision, synthesis agreed outcome

Figure 4-7   Example of a Rich Picture for Action Learning Cycle 2 from the Founder of an NZ/Australian/USA NGO working in Indonesia

This is followed by the third rich picture (Figure 4-7), from the founder of a Non-Governmental Organization (NGO) based in Indonesia who carried out significant recovery work in the Indonesian islands most devastated by both the tsunami and the subsequent earthquake. This rich picture, although rendered by someone from a vastly different worldview and position, also sums up similar aspects of sharing and, in this case, leading the vision and values, and planning and progress monitoring to achieve sustainable outcomes. It also notes the need for kindness, trust, respect, and even love. It sees success as "getting people with the same vision on the same path." By now, one may see emerging synergies and convergence between the points brought out by each of these respondents. Such similarities only got stronger as more rich pictures were created.

Figure 4-8 illustrates the fourth rich picture, which was developed by Paul and the Australian Chief Operations Officer (COO) of an NGO involved in the post-disaster programs. The COO was working partly in Indonesia, but mostly out of headquarters in Australia.

A number of key points emerged from these eight developed rich pictures; some were repeated across all eight, while others were more characteristic of the particular circumstances of the programs, purpose, local environment, or context of the picture's creator.

It is nevertheless illuminating to draw out particular points from some of these rich pictures. Figure 4-5 highlights trust, sensitizing in the local context, empathizing, and understanding. Figure 4-7 cites the sharing and leading of the

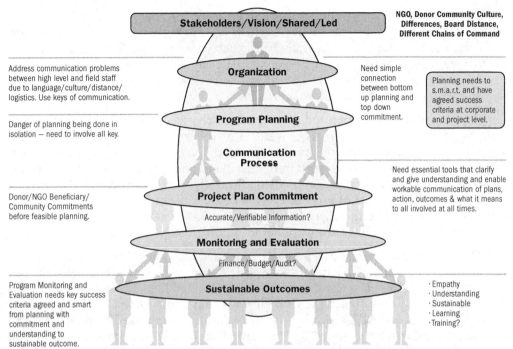

Figure 4-8 Example of a Rich Picture for Action Learning Cycle 2 from a COO of Health NGO Based out of Australia into Indonesia

vision of the program as a key factor. Interestingly, overall leadership did not feature as a key success factor from the eight rich pictures. It certainly was seen as an issue, but the methods, communication, and outcome management were more often depicted as key factors. Figure 4-7 also addresses kindness, trust, love, and other aspects, which did not appear as strongly in other rich pictures, but are nevertheless understood to be important. These issues also fall into the frames of leadership and emotional intelligence, as reviewed in Chapter 2, Sections 2.7.1 to 2.7.3.

Emerging more consistently as background issues were empathy, leadership, trust, confidence, and culture. It is therefore important that we do not lose sight of such factors, and it is also why we explored so deeply the philosophical underpinnings of our methodology and outcomes. A key to our understanding here is that critical reality sometimes runs the risk of not recognizing these issues sufficiently, whereas praxis and pragmatism could incorporate them more readily and workably.

Figure 4-8 probably sums up the collection of rich pictures. The key steps or factors drawn out here relate to the importance of stakeholder engagement, objectives sharing and organization, program planning, the communication process, and achieving an effective balance between top-down commitment and bottom-up planning. It also brings out the need for commitment to the project plan and the keys of monitoring and evaluation to sustainable outcomes. Once again, it draws attention to empathy, understanding, and learning, while not representing them as key factors. It also raises the question of leadership.

The full collection of rich pictures can be seen in Appendix 5 of Paul's thesis. All the pictures reward our scrutiny, for they certainly elicited much more understanding and structured insight than ever expected by anyone. The interviews and extensive notes were reviewed with each participant separately and confidentially. The key levels of factors, as agreed within those reviews, were then interpreted into three layers on the pictures in a general sense.

The background graphics and pictures were the *what* of the relating, the captions were the background to the needs, and the key steps they saw extracted were the "keys" to the method and *how to*, or the need and the resolution of such experience and how they may work in reality. *What* and *how* questions are, as noted in Section 3.3.4, critical to action learning. Initially, it was not intended to review these in separate layers; that process evolved because of the interest and subsequent questioning of some of the rich picture partners as they sought to clarify what it meant to them and their future work before signing off.

This layering and extraction actually generated more significant value than expected by any of the respondents, Paul (who felt very challenged by just getting out to all these far-flung places and very busy people, striving to translate what they saw and told, and then finalizing rich pictures that actually worked for them), or his PhD supervisors. All participants were eventually impressed by how clear the alignments and outcomes were. The extraction of the layering of each rich picture and its aligning factors can be seen in Appendix 5 of his thesis.

What also proved very valuable through the refinement of this SSM approach was the use of the natural precedence of colors, which has been realized in other arts and sciences, in the development of the sequencing and flow through the various timings and precedence of an antecedent and project development. Hence, rather than a simple flow chart connected by logical input to output systematic positivist type arrows (which most of these kinds of operators just don't work with and saw as being too rigid or mechanistic), the same sense of precedence and flow, but with less fixed rigidity, was developed through the intelligent use of colors—as an artist would deploy and develop them on a canvas.

These colors also have synergies relating to their internationally-recognized representations of concepts such as danger, growth, communication, safety, and wisdom (see Figure 4-9). Having a protocol for that more general understanding

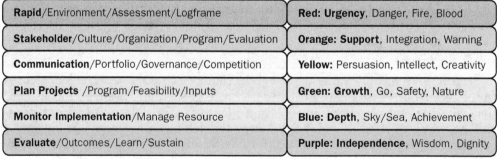

Rapid/Environment/Assessment/Logframe	**Red: Urgency**, Danger, Fire, Blood
Stakeholder/Culture/Organization/Program/Evaluation	**Orange: Support**, Integration, Warning
Communication/Portfolio/Governance/Competition	**Yellow:** Persuasion, Intellect, Creativity
Plan Projects /Program/Feasibility/Inputs	**Green: Growth**, Go, Safety, Nature
Monitor Implementation/Manage Resource	**Blue: Depth**, Sky/Sea, Achievement
Evaluate/Outcomes/Learn/Sustain	**Purple: Independence**, Wisdom, Dignity

Figure 4-9   Example of a Rich Picture for Action Learning Cycle 2 Color Coding for Emotions

and feeling for emotions meant that Paul was able to enhance the development of the order of outcomes, or the more human understanding and development of sequences, both in background and key factor, front-end process, and resolution.

The strong synergies that developed in order and process through the eight rich pictures, in terms of key factors, made the identification of recurring themes (keys), in both antecedent and the project intellectual and emotional framework (frame), unexpectedly clear. The process for drawing out those keys was not difficult because each of the rich pictures had been purposefully drawn in a planned layering form, with background factors themselves embedded in the actual pictures to give context. Relating the issues and their needs was embedded in the captions of each rich picture, and personal or observed key steps were made explicit in the actual elliptical-shaped process steps, as illustrated in Figure 4-10. From each rich picture, the key steps in particular were extracted and compared, and the repeating synergies or most recurrent steps were mapped to a summary flow process, with an alignment in color and sequence evolving from it.

This color coding was never seen as an end in itself, nor as crucial to the research, but it certainly did enable a less threatening and more flexible arrival at key process order and communication. The value of the color sequence resonated with all the participants (regardless of their national or organizational cultural background), and even with Western practitioners in the peer review who had a predominantly "hard" or traditional project management worldview. This approach was also seen to enable color coding for rapidly locating what decisions have to be made and by whom and was then enacted through a process of sense-making in post

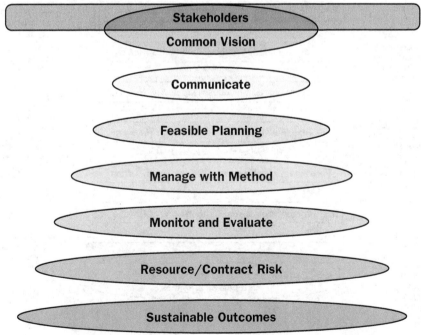

Figure 4-10   Example of Typical Key Steps to Factors Extractions

disaster response and categorization. This approach is not unlike the color coding that enables purposeful enactment in hospital emergency rooms.

As this approach to developing rich pictures evolved (for these key participants), it proved as important as, if not more important than, the words and processes that followed. Many of the participants later told Paul that working through this process actually clarified their view of their own perspective and experience and gave them clearer insight into, and understanding of, their project management practice. They believed it would undoubtedly enhance their future project participation. They expressed as much gratitude for being involved as did Paul for their willingness to be involved.

It has been part of Paul's project paradigm that project management is part art, part science, and, in previous project planning developments, in both the "hard" and "soft" worlds. The use of colors and the idea of their natural understandings, as well as process developments, are integral to developing a pragmatic working resolution for practical outcomes. This constitutes further evidence of his paradigm, where sense-making is enacted through being a bricoleur and pragmatically using whatever useful tools can be fashioned out of objects at hand (Weick, 1988; 1995a).

The key steps for each of the eight pictures were extracted (see Appendix 5 in Steinfort, 2010), at which point the very strong synergies became abundantly clear. This represented a form of saturation of results so that we could be confident that the insights revealed were valid and useful. One such extraction, illustrated in Figure 4-11, typifies the key factors review. The alignment and synergy of key factor

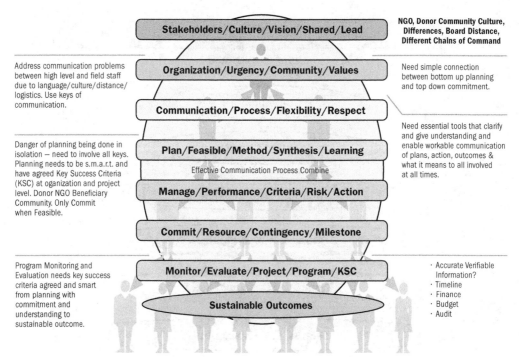

Figure 4-11   Summary of Key Factors and Issues Repeated from Eight Rich Pictures

results, evident from this approach, led to a clear, high-level view of the research results. This was mainly because the process was derived from clear agreement between participants in developing the key rich picture from the disaster zones and their experience with recovery and reconstruction programs. This then enabled strong convergence and agreement on the root definition development.

It is worthwhile reflecting on the overall review of the rich pictures, as they brought so much more understanding about the nature and importance of the key identified factors, issues, and indeed the what, who, why, and how of the antecedents of project management practice.

What emerged from the rich pictures illustrated in Figure 4-5, Figure 4-6, Figure 4-7, Figure 4-8, and Figure 4-11 was the consistency between the key steps or factors that were repeated throughout most, if not all, of those pictures. This was also identified in reviews of each of the rich pictures featured in the body of Paul's thesis (refer to Appendix 5 in Steinfort, 2010).

Factors identified and presented in Figure 4-5 are as follows:

stakeholder engagement > leading through shared vision/objectives

organization > the need for urgency and flexibility in communication based on community and respect for values

program and project planning > using feasible methods, pragmatic synthesis of approaches, and learning from experience

managing > performance judged by sensible criteria that can be made sense of; managing risk and managing appropriate action taken

commitment > committing adequate resources and contingencies; being committed to milestones

monitoring and evaluation > toward sustainable outcomes

Although these preceding factors did not feature as key criteria in this rich picture set of engagements, they did draw on the realization of the need for leadership, trust, empathy, and other social and emotional aspects, which may then call for authentic leadership as outlined earlier in Chapter 2, Section 2.7.3. Leadership, authentic or otherwise, and the emotional intelligence of the project managers were recognized as important elements of the disaster recovery program outcome, but it was not always possible to ensure such a level of leadership. It was seen that issues of integrity, ethical and authentic leadership, and emotional and social intelligence are parts of the *why* question of the action learning situational analysis. Leadership could even be embedded in the process, rather than relying on whoever may or may not have what it takes in terms of ethics and leadership in the challenging contexts and programs.

4.4.2.2   SSM–Developing a Root Definition Model of the Messy Situation

In a standard SSM approach, the step that follows the development of rich pictures is the construction of a model. This model describes a system that can be used to address the messy situation. It provides a set of links to subsystems connected to the situation by stepping back into the "real" (as opposed to "system") world to analyze the rich pictures' data, exposed themes, and issues. The outcome of that process is what is called a *root definition*—i.e., the development of models to deal with and address the identified messy problem that triggered the SSM process. Readers may wish to refresh their memory of the seven-step SSM process by referring to Section 3.3.2, and Figure 3-1 in particular.

The root definition is guided by a mnemonic—CATWOE. It is a finely crafted statement of the "messy" problem in terms of the following:

C   Clients, who would be the victims/beneficiaries of the purposeful activity

A   Actors, who would perform (do) the activities

T   Transformation process–the purposeful activity expressed as an input > Transformation > output

W   Worldview, or point of view that makes this definition meaningful

O   Owner–owner or stopper of this purposeful activity

E   Environment–constraints in its environment that this system takes as given

In a project management sense, the root definition can provide the project with a realistic scope statement and a model for action to address the identified problem. We felt that this could be a valuable tool in the traditional project management briefing process and, indeed, we did see in the literature some isolated calls for SSM to be used in project management at the briefing stage (Green & Simister, 1999; Winter & Checkland, 2003; Checkland & Winter, 2006; Winter, 2009), and also for undertaking value engineering studies during the project design stage (Green, 1999).

This CATWOE respects the needs of key stakeholders for any program, action research, or general community project process. Three of the elements in CATWOE relate to people/stakeholder issues—clients, actors, and owners. One possible reason why SSM has proven so popular amongst project research professionals is that it at least leads the communication through the essential people to some agreed on and workable set of outcomes.

We suggest that traditional project management, at least in the way it is captured in the *PMBOK® Guide*, does not deeply expose people to either stakeholder engagement theory or practice, despite an enhanced focus in the most recent version of the *PMBOK® Guide* (PMI, 2008a). Value is also an aspect that is not very extensively addressed in the *PMBOK® Guide*. At least the SSM process and mnemonic CATWOE does discipline researchers to address people and stakeholder issues in messy situations.

Stakeholder engagement guides people through a number of *who* enquiries:

who holds the power or ownership?

who has the influence?

who are the beneficiaries?

who is in alignment?, etc.

This is presently a poorly addressed aspect of *PMBOK® Guide*-type project management processes, and while *The Standard for Program Management* (PMI, 2006b) and *The Standard for Portfolio Management* (PMI, 2006a) have more recently attempted to address this deficiency, they still read like "bolt-on after-work" treatment of these important management areas, rather than integral front-ends or antecedents needed to enable project management best practice.

Checkland (2000; Checkland & Winter, 2006) resolved to adopt a simpler four-step process in the later stages of SSM theory and implementation development, and he reviewed an alternative mnemonic to CATWOE in the adapted SSM process. He summarized this alternative, or optional process, as a series of questions:

What to do? (P)

How to do it? (Q)

Why do it? (R)

However, this does not address the key parties in the stakeholder engagement process. The danger here is that project managers using this simpler four-step process may lose the advantage of developing a root definition that is ensured by using CATWOE and its necessary stakeholder engagement process.

The root definition development is, however, similar to Dick's (2009) "situation analysis" to describe outcomes and actions. SSM, as stated earlier, is a function of action research, so they go hand-in-glove.

The framing of the CATWOE root definition leads to the processing of the models for resolution with respect to a greater understanding of both the proposed problem situation and its solution. Steps 1 and 2 in the seven-step process are set in the "real world" environment. Steps 3 and 4 have the flexibility and freedom of being addressed in the ideal or systems environment, which brings the advantage of being able to develop and improve the philosophical frame of reference and models until these best resemble the environment they are being designed for.

This process of enhancement, in and out of the "real" to the "ideal," comes from systems thinking, both in open and closed systems theory. However, this SSM approach is not unique to either systems or SSM theory and implementation. Project planning precedes Gantt by a century, and was used even earlier in civil engineering and other design and building projects, possibly as far back as the pyramids (Morris, 1994). It is best to operate within theory, and to model proposed problem solutions before attempting to put them into practice, so that potential problems can be anticipated and addressed before they emerge "out of thin air."

There is a palpable advantage to this "real" to "ideal" SSM approach of model development and testing before implementation. Indeed, the process proved very valuable in the second stage of our research by helping us, and other key players, to identify the antecedents of project management best practice. However, while this SSM approach was deemed a valuable, though demanding, process by respondents engaged in this action learning stage and Paul's CoP (who provided continual feedback on its progress and evolution), feedback from these groups indicated that the time demands and rigor of SSM might not necessarily work for the majority of project people in the field.

The following *root definition* was enacted for understanding a post-disaster scenario:

A group/project/manager has to rapidly assess the feasibility of competing projects for a community after a disaster or for general aid/relief. This is done for, and in conjunction with, a group of stakeholders to scope, plan, and implement (if feasible) a program or project to enable disaster preparedness or recovery/reconstruction to a set of sustainable outcomes.

CATWOE Key Sentences

Client: Community, Donor.

Actors: Stakeholders, i.e., NGO, Donor, Community, Local Government, Project Manager, Aid Partners.

Transformation: Tangible and Intangible–Infrastructure/Shelter/Security/Livelihood/Knowledge, Process, Trust, Support, Empathy, Understanding, Sustainable and Safe Future.

Weltanschauung (Worldview): Because there is an urgent and desperate need to assess the achievability of planning and implementing an emergency preparedness/recovery/reconstruction/livelihood project or program, does it align with the need and group objectives? Who are the key and reliable stakeholders? Can it be resourced, and will it achieve a sustainable outcome?

Owner: Project/Program Manager (for) Donor/NGO/Community (Key Stakeholders).

Environment: Poor, under-resourced, possibly desperate or endemic context, urgent needs, demanding, and possibly hostile environment, need for long- and short-term goals.

To enable a group/temporary organization of Community, Donor(s), NGO(s)/ project manager to assess, scope, plan, agree, commit to, and implement (from competing projects) an appropriate and feasible program for a community after a disaster or for relief/recovery/reconstruction/sustainable outcomes and a Safe Future for that Community.

The eight rich pictures drawn from the participants' experiences in post-tsunami and post-earthquake projects showed very strong convergence. Even more striking was their synergy with the key steps emerging from both the earlier literature review of a range of projects and Paul's reflections upon his project management practice experience related in Action Research Cycle 1 Reflections, as discussed in Section 4.3.3.

This root definition is summarized in Figure 4-12 in the form of a flow chart or, in traditional project management terms, a work breakdown structure.

4.4.2.3 SSM–Action to Improve the Messy Situation
We argue that the SSM, either in its summary form (and especially where understandable and interested stakeholder engagement is to be enabled) as outlined in

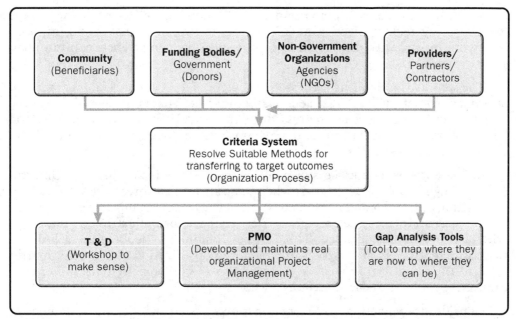

Figure 4-12   Root Definition for the Research Summary Rich Picture

Figure 4-13, or in its full seven-step form, suggests that stakeholder engagement and planning project management activities warrant more serious and rigorous consideration. The researched SSM process highlighted the need for necessary, but flexible, stakeholder assessment and scoping to achieve sustainable outcomes. This proposition was supported by feedback from key players in the field, managing such large programs through analysis of the eight rich pictures and synthesis within the context of the root definition arrived at, and strongly validated, by the study participants.

A set of project management actions was synthesized from the SSM root definition process and is presented in Figure 4-13. The key to successful organizations,

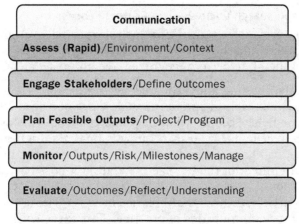

Figure 4-13   Summative Rich Picture Antecedent and Project Key Concepts

programs, and projects in any environment is in knowing how to enable the process to *plan, do,* and *review* objective outcomes in the environment that the organization is to work in, and with due regard to communication, competence, commitment, and consequent risk.

The steps in the planning process for each level (i.e., at the project, program, and organization strategic levels) are generically the same. That is, we need to break the objective into key items to be progressed and then to review their value and risk and how they are related at the project to program stage through core values, in order to see where the necessary fit is achieved.

In itself, the generic process of *plan, do,* and *review* is not difficult. Unfortunately though, it does get confusing when there are at least three different ontological positions through combinations of views, by levels of organizations, programs, and projects and where the core process or sequence for evaluating the necessary criteria is not well understood. This can be simplified by looking at each of the three different levels of a project-to-program-to-organization vision achievement through the same intrinsic series of steps with the different actions and criteria connections, which enable success as a whole.

Consider the enabling of an organization's vision, which is a statement of the future realization. That vision is planned through the core values to arrive at key strategies to maintain the vision over time. Programs to generate these outcomes will be aligned according to the *fit, value,* and *risk* factors and then enabled by planning them through projects. A program is a broad effort encompassing a number of projects, and each project is also enabled through a plan, this time through key steps aligned with timelined outcomes and with allowance for risk and reward. There needs to be an objective means of defining program and project priority, every program should specify the projects that will allow for its attainment, and every project should directly align with, and support the delivery of, the strategic plan.

The synthesis and resolution of these processes can then be developed into the following conceptual model for solution implementation, illustrated in Figure 4-14.

4.4.3 Action Research Cycle 2—The Reflect Process

Paul's findings provided a significant and unexpectedly rewarding opportunity for both the researcher and the researched practitioners, as well as project management practice in general, to better recognize project management best practice.

First, a strongly aligning and validated set of key antecedent and project factors was identified and resolved amongst a wide range of respected and experienced practitioners in the field. Second, what had emerged from this cycle was the realization that the antecedents (at least in international aid, higher risk zones) had a greater effect than had been understood by any previous work in this area. Third, the unexpected alignment of the key factors and their possible categorization into a three-level solution (i.e., organization, to program, to project), actually brought more due process to this research than if it had been set within the more traditional *PMBOK® Guide*-type communities of practice. This three-level ontology has been

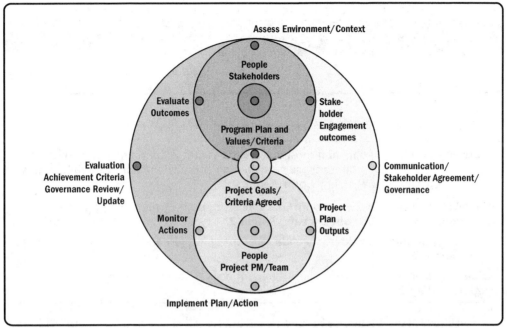

Figure 4-14   Synthesis of Project Program Organization Process in Balance of Nature in an Eastern Yin-Yang Graphic Format

the natural way in which a lot of field practice has been developed throughout the history of LogFrame and project cycle management.

We initially thought we would be taking lessons from the traditional project management world *to* these aid project practitioners—not receiving significant lessons *from* them. The reason for this unexpected result is self-evident once one has time to reflect upon it. These international aid projects, from their inception to their completion, are considerably more exposed to changing events, environment, politics, risk, and less stability than traditional projects. Hence, although it is not immediately obvious, these projects and practitioners have had to develop processes that are more open at the project front end, if they are to better consider problems and solutions and to better cope with changing conditions and situations. LogFrame is notably better at the "front end" of projects than *PMBOK® Guide* and has been functioning in that role for over 40 years, whereas *PMBOK® Guide* is better in stable conditions where the "front end" is mostly set.

Work developed in the first research phase, then provided input into this second action learning cycle through a reasonably straightforward process of working through the root definitions and the three-level overview and synergistic perspectives to the interconnected cycles illustrated and summarized in Figure 4-8. The synthesis of the organization-to-program-to-project interconnected cycles benefited from the action research and project/program alignments, also realized earlier in this study. They provided a focusing and aligning philosophical framework for addressing the next action learning cycle.

Table 4-4   Criteria Assessment for Action Research Learning Cycle 2

Knowledge, Understanding, and Sense-Making	Workable Practice	Community Internal and External Validation	Value to Outcome Impact
4	3	3	3
Effective sense-making	Effective	Effective	Objective impact and value

The following provides greater detail for the ratings given in Table 4-4:

Knowledge, understanding, and sense-making–These results and findings were clearly significant and of value both to those participating and further, more generally, in this aid/project project management world. *Rating 4*

Workable practice–These were confirmed in practice both through the participating practitioners and through other means. *Rating 3*

Community internal and external validation–Strong interest and supportive response all round. *Rating 3*

Value to outcome impact–Significant value, but not yet completed in process and method. *Rating 3*

The above assessment was further tested and/or validated by a completely different set of experienced practitioners from those who participated in the SSM exercise. Some of them were part of Paul's CoP. This validation of the second action research cycle was enabled by communication of review and reflection (summative) results from the rich-picture SSM process, while undertaking a forward review (formative) and reflection exercise with project management practitioners from a broader set of traditional project management industry sectors than the aid/relief project world rich-picture participants.

This validation workshop was held at a suitably reflective venue—the Melbourne Cricket Ground (MCG) Executive Suite, overlooking one of the most famous sporting venues in the world. This venue was also chosen because Paul was the project manager responsible for its $430 million redevelopment to hold the 2006 Commonwealth Games, and his PSA practice had won the 2006 Australian Institute of Project Management (AIPM) Project Management Achievement Award for stakeholder satisfaction and successful outcomes of a major community project. The venue, its history, and its symbolism as a tangible example of acknowledged project management best practice formed the backdrop for the review and critique of what was developed by aid project managers through the SSM process.

The participants who joined Paul and Derek in the MCG workshop were:

1. Program Manager for a national communications and technology group (30 years project experience)
2. Project Director for local government (30 years organization, program, and project experience)
3. Engineering Manager for an international petroleum consortium responsible for large refinery programs and projects (40 years organization, program, and project experience)
4. International Development Project Management Consultant (35 years project and program experience)

5. Program Planning Management Practitioner responsible for major local and national projects in government and private practice (22 years organization, program, and project experience)
6. Project Management Practitioner working mainly on major building projects (8 years experience)
7. Project Training Practitioner (10 years project experience)
8. Project Practitioner–projects and programs (3 years experience)
9. Project Program and Project Consultant Practitioner (6 years experience)
10. Project Program and Project Consultant Practitioner (30 years experience)

The preparation for this workshop first addressed the questions of who was most appropriate for peer review, how the participants would be briefed and prepared for the workshop, and what the necessary followup would be. Participants were mostly practitioners working on a range of projects in Australia, including overseas aid projects, though none had participated in the rich-picture SSM exercise. This group had held roles as program managers in major Australian organizations, project managers from traditional design and construction backgrounds, group managers, project field coordinators, and other project management roles and academic positions. They were forwarded key factor outcome summaries and possible solutions/processes for models and feasible resulting action, and they were invited to reflect upon these documents and prepare their responses as workshop participants.

The actual workshop day consisted of an introductory reflection upon the road less travelled to that point, an outline of general understandings of project management success, and an overview of the antecedents of project success. It also involved some reflection upon the very different environment of the workshop, compared with that of post-disaster projects and the aid/development world in general. Work teams were formed to review, critique, and provide feedback suggestions on each set of key factors for each possible project phase. Some valuable modifications were agreed on, mainly in the need for definition/terminology of each of the key terms used. This confusion arose because different sectors may have traditions of different understandings for words such as "program," "environment," and others.

This workshop, while being very valuable in its review and reflection, and containing some very respected and seasoned practitioners, did not markedly change any of the key factor findings. One significant outcome of this effort was that most of the attendees found the day itself valuable and informative, thus reinforcing the need to understand these emerging antecedents of project management best practice in the context of the rapidly-changing world they all faced.

Whereas Paul and Derek had originally expected that the traditional project management world practice would be imparting wisdom to the project management aid project world practitioners (operating in their high-risk, poorer, and disaster prone areas), the ironic realization dawned on all workshop participants that, in fact, traditional project management practitioners had much to learn from the project management aid project world practitioners. The experience gained from the SSM engagement highlighted that the methods which aid project world practitioners had developed over decades had much to offer in helping us better understand the antecedents of project management practice in challenging environments.

We expected that the MCG workshop would change and challenge our research findings to that point. What we discovered was that our findings from the disaster-response fields of Asia actually impressed and challenged these seasoned project management practitioners more than they, or we, expected. In fact they were thankful for the exposure to this knowledge. It was then that the significance of the focus on the antecedents of project management success began to become more evident to us, to the wider workshop group, and to traditional project management in general.

Another positive outcome from the workshop was that, through reflection, the explanation of terms used in the project management best practice antecedents illustrated in Figure 4-7, Summative Rich Picture Antecedent and Project Key Concepts, became more refined and clearer, as follows:

Environment –the natural world, especially as affected by human organization/activity.

Organization –an organized body of people with a particular purpose.

Purpose –the reason for which something is done or for which something exists; resolve or determination.

Program–a broad effort encompassing a number of projects and/or functional activities with a common purpose.

Stakeholder–a person with an interest or stake in the organization.

Culture –customs, institutions, and achievements of a particular nation, people, or group.

Values –principles, standards, or qualities considered worthwhile or desirable.

Success Criteria (CSC)–the standards by which the project is to be judged to have been successful in the eyes of the stakeholders.

Communication–the exchange of information, ideas, or feelings—a plan of the communications activities during the program.

Governance–the functions, responsibilities, processes, and procedures that define how the program is set up, managed, and controlled.

Competence–having the necessary skill or knowledge to do something successfully.

Trust –firm belief in the reliability, truth, ability, or strength of someone or something.

Intangible Goals–goals that are not directly quantifiable but that should still be built into the program or project where possible, e.g., improvements in staff learning.

Program Management–the coordinated organization, direction, and implementation of a portfolio of projects and activities that together achieve outcomes and realize benefits that are of strategic importance.

Project–a temporary organization to undertake a unique, novel, and transient endeavor managing the inherent uncertainty and need for integration in order to deliver beneficial objectives of change.

Plan(ning)–a scheme, program, or method worked out beforehand for the accomplishment of an objective.

Implement–put into effect.

Monitor –keep under observation, especially so as to regulate, record, or control.

Outcome–results or changes of the program or a process, including outputs, effects, and impacts.

Critical Success Factors (CSF)–these are key areas of activity or enablers with which favorable results are necessary for a group to reach its goal.

Evaluate–to decide the value or worth of.

Benefits–quantitative and qualitative improvements expected or resulting from a plan or program.

Stakeholder Expectations–what is considered the most likely to happen. Any expectation is a belief that is centered on the future, and which may or may not be realistic.

Evaluation Criteria–measurable indicators that will be used to evaluate the progress or otherwise toward agreed (tangible and intangible) outcomes and long-term desired impacts.

Value–relative worth, merit, or importance.

This led to a review and reframing of a model to illustrate a more rigorous project program development process by reference to 12 identified factors of project management best practice. This was conceptualized from an action learning paradigm (Kolb, 1984), presented at the beginning of this chapter as a four-stage cycle of *evaluation, planning, action,* and *reviewing.* The irony is that we returned to an action learning view of project management best practice—though perhaps subconsciously so—simply *because of* our pragmatic philosophical position and ontological stance as practicing project managers and "pracademics" with a view of pragmatic foundations of epistemology. Figure 4-15 illustrates the outcome developed from the validation and reflection MCG workshop that best represents its conclusions.

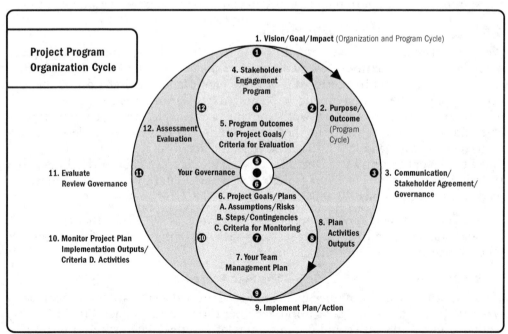

Figure 4-15   Project Program Organization Cycle Showing a 12-Key Factor Process

Table 4-5   Criteria Assessment for Action Research Learning Cycle 2

Knowledge, Understanding, and Sense-Making	Workable Practice	Community Internal and External Validation	Value to Outcome Impact
4	3	4	3
Effective sense-making	Effective	Very effective	Impact and value

The value of these realizations and understandings was again extensive and possibly even more surprising. It was not expected that mainstream project management practitioners would so clearly validate and further integrate these factors into their working method. Several of the participants in this workshop provided feedback and further input and reinforcement that helped us feel comfortable that some form of saturation of the action learning cycle outcomes was at hand.

The following provides greater detail on the ratings given in Table 4-4, which updates Table 4-3. Valuable understanding was achieved from all of this work and reinforced by practitioners as reliable practice and, in nearly all cases, the participants stated they had learned a lot from the workshop and could then see the antecedent and project management integration. In both this workshop and the interactions with the practitioners in the aid/relief world, members of the respective communities of practice all appreciated and worked with those findings. The impact of this work on the key research objective was seen as very valuable and certainly worth pursuing in the field. This led to the third and final action learning cycle, in which reframed and revised project management models were tested in the field within a particularly turbulent and challenging aid/recovery context—this time on our home front, rather than in remote lands and addressing distant disasters.

4.5 Action Learning Cycle Three

We used our models and understanding in a real-life and very immediate program of projects in the bushfire recovery effort after the devastating February 2009 fires in Victoria. As stated in Section 4.2 of this chapter and highlighted in Table 2-1, outcome 3, we intended to produce a pragmatic project management process to be used in crisis situations which would provide a workable, improved, understandable and meaningful process to those addressing the exigencies in doing project management work (action 3.2). This cycle would also test our ideas *in vivo*, and so allow us the opportunity to investigate any further convergence of thinking about the antecedents of project management best practice and to further summarize a workable model (actions 3.2 and 3.3 in Table 2-1).

We document here how we undertook this cycle, as with the other two cycles, using action learning in three subsections—the planning process, the act-observe process, and then reflection and evaluation.

4.5.1 Action Research Cycle 3—The Plan Process

While the research findings had received significant validation and support, it was still questionable, in Paul's mind, whether the evolving model was sufficiently workable in communities and communities of practice. The process made sense from an overall perspective, but how to make it work effectively through a range of environments, contexts, and people was, to a significant extent, an unanswered question. The Director of the Department of Planning and Community Development in our home state of Victoria approached Paul for assistance and advice in response to an urgent and perceived need to improve the project management of the bushfire response. This provided a unique opportunity to test the Action Research Cycle 2 results in practice. Cycle 3 progressed, and continued to validate, the results gained from the participants of the previous SSM and validation work reported in Action Research Cycle 2.

The interesting challenge from this government department, not necessarily new to Paul's professional project management practice, was to effect a three-level approach through the *strategic > program > project* levels and their various linkages, interacting processes, and criteria. This engagement in particular led to further work being seen as necessary to initially model and get effective understanding and ownership of the process and work at the different levels.

This is where lessons from the previous cycle added some extra insights to that front-end strategic thinking about how a top-down, overarching organizational leadership strategy can be understood and framed in ways that can be readily transferred at the program level and then to the project level, so that the clarity of vision and evaluation measures for monitoring and evaluation remain usable and workable at the program level. Then it is a matter of integrating that understanding into the more readily understood (by the traditional project management community) areas of planning and monitoring for project planning, organization, and control.

The principal point of departure from a traditional project management context was the adaptation of LogFrame to better establish the program phase and adaptation of M&E from the aid world as a useful tool. Linking these two aid world tools to the traditional project management tools and techniques enabled better scoped project tasks and activities. Figure 4-16 was developed as a useful way to visualize the planned approach that was developed for the work comprising Action Research Work Cycle 3. It should be stressed that this was a *live* testing of the approach.

The February 2009 Victorian bushfires had ravaged and destroyed whole communities and left many survivors traumatized, in the same way Hurricane Katrina had done in the United States or the December 2004 tsunami had done in Indonesia. In fact, Paul's sister was a victim, her home having been destroyed by the bushfires. This context is important, as it illustrates the seriousness and rigor with which the action cycle took place. Validity is focused upon by answering a series of questions through researching organizations using action research (Eden & Huxham, 2006) and the cyclic action (Kemmis & McTaggart, 1988; Hope & Waterman, 2003). Thus, research, joint action, and reflexivity (Shalin, 1992) are developed with each refining cycle through the evaluation of the planned outcomes and their impact on the overall goal or objective. This is the key to understanding the validity of undertaking action cycles and whether further action and evaluation add value.

Paul's approach was embraced by the Victorian Bushfire Reconstruction and Recovery Authority (VBRRA), and it has since been used in over 120 projects.

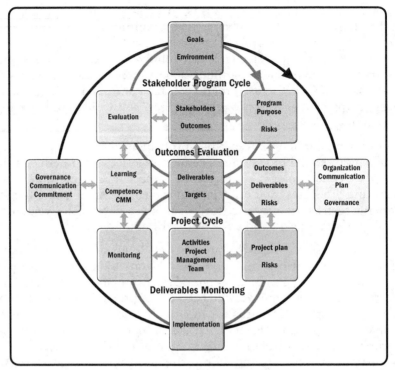

Figure 4-16   Full View of Overall Organization to Program
to Project Cycle Management Process

4.5.2   Action Research Cycle 3—The Act-Observe Process

The three-level project-to-program-to-organization cycle was put into practice and underwent testing and evaluation in both the local situation and the overall general interpretation of the working experience of the post-bushfire response in Victoria. The following summary of the process of the three cycles working together was developed through further development of the action research, to arrive at the best methodology to accomplish this aim. This brought together the program cycle management in a step-by-step process, with each main step broken down into further detailed steps, as illustrated in Figure 4-15. This methodology enabled everyone, especially managers, to see relationships and links between different levels of the overall organization, but at the same time to see their place in the overall system and how and where their actions fit in.

This approach is very similar to the standard work breakdown structure approach of traditional project management where one works with main framework summaries and then, for each of those, more detailed activities fit within each particular element of that framework. This main cycle summary framework, with more detailed actities to be checked off or enacted, was found by the range of practitioners and the community in general to be the most workable when applied to these projects and their now recognized antecedents.

Figure 4-15 illustrates the clear steps and links between each of the processes to be followed, so that people can focus on their area and identify what steps or processes fit (or are available to them), while at the same time they can see dependency relationships with any other elements they or others may be engaged in. This model was best understood by managers who could then see who needed to do what and how to do it. It also provided logical order and sequence in activities and resolution so that people felt much clearer about the scope of what they and their organization were to do, and they also had a reference for understanding the actions or processes that belonged to each step or section of the project program organization cycles. Each step or square has certain processes and requirements which then lead to the next step in logical order and through each cycle, to realize the outcomes needed. For instance, the resolution of stakeholder outcomes (the orange square in the stakeholder program cycle) leads to the targeting of deliverables (the light brown square at the center of the figure). This square lies at the linkage of the program and project cycles. This deliverable then leads to the need for certain competencies in the blue "learning" square. These competiencies could very well include not only traditional project management skills, but also emotional intelligence and authentic leadership competencies. The process of goals > outcomes > deliverable activities > project plan constantly referred to can be seen within this graphic, clearly embedded in both the three-cycle process and the LogFrame steps.

This proved very valuable in the overview and for those at a high management level to understand and make decisions on process, policy, and governance. At the same time, however, it possibly provided information overload for those at the project's "coal face" level. What evolved from this realization was the need to keep steps simple, focused, and uncomplicated. As such, in order to maximize commitment at the working level, the key steps were made clear and the key aspects of how to meaningfully and effectively identify and engage with key stakeholders, to resolve the key outcomes to achieve the program or organization objective from their "point of view," and then to plan the activities and address the risks to achieving these objectives were recognized. Again, the synergy and alignment of the project to program management and the action to research dual working cycles came through. The ongoing and increasingly validating resolution of these becoming the same key steps was apparent.

While a series of "normal" traditional project management tools and techniques were used (where the situation facing VBRRA was seen to be consistent with "earth" type projects and where it could pragmatically be seen to do so), aid world tools such as LogFrame linked to a more conventional, traditional project management world tool were successfully used at the project front end and at the program level. The overall systems map illustrated in Figure 4-15 was used as a linking and communication device to help participants in this somewhat chaotic, and at times frenetic, process of responding to the rebuild effort. Two devices or tools were used over the 9- to 12-month time frame in which the action learning cycle which is reported on in this book took place. The first one, as illustrated in Table 4-6, is a LogFrame tool application.

This tool clearly identifies the goal, expected outcome, output, and activities needed to achieve the goal. The second device, illustrated in Figure 4-17, is a traditional project management tool, the work breakdown structure (WBS) that linked to the front end high level LogFrame tool.

Table 4-6   Horizontal Alignment of Goals to Outcomes to Outputs

Goal	Outcome	Output	Activity
To Rebuild a Village Community	Infrastructure in Place and Working	Social Infrastructure	Community Hubs Case Workers Contingency
		Civil Infrastructure	Assess Design Construction Contingency
		Power	
		Amenity	
	Community Facilities Rebuilt	First Community Facility	Needs Design Construction Operation Contingency

The use of color coding consistent with the organization-to-program-to-project Cycle Management Process model illustrated in Figure 4-16 was also used as an innovation. M&E approaches from the aid/project world were also used to monitor program outcomes and outputs indicated in the LogFrame illustrated in Table 4-6. While it is beyond the scope of this book to provide details of how this phase of the PhD research was conducted, readers should refer to Paul's thesis for further information.

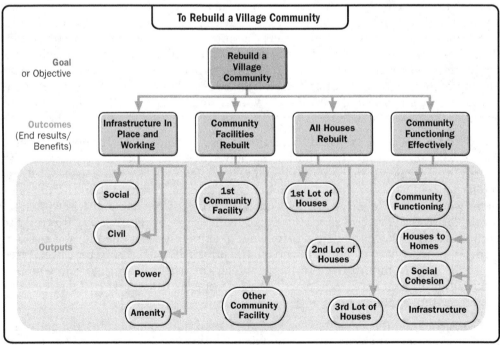

Figure 4-17   Working Example of Typical WBS Triangulated Through Logic of Outputs to Outcomes to Objective Impact

4.5.3 Action Research Cycle 3—The Reflect Process

As noted earlier (Chapter 2, Section 2.7.2.) the stakeholder engagement process is one of the least used, but most needed, in traditional project management, despite recent changes to the *PMBOK® Guide* (PMI, 2008a) and several recent studies and papers relating to this aspect. Our study so far on the antecedents of effective and successful project management processes also highlights the essential place of stakeholder engagement in projects. It is probably one of the most important findings of Paul's PhD thesis, as it is of other related doctoral studies (for example, Bourne, 2005; Aaltonen et al., 2008; and Aaltonen & Sivonen, 2009). Effective stakeholder engagement is not a quick fix. It is an arduous process to engage stakeholders in a way that brings out what is needed for project success, but does not leave them without adequate representation, understanding, and appropriate outcomes through the engagement.

What typically happens in these situations is that there is some nominal interchange through the project scoping, but questions of who in the community represents what interests, and whether they truly represent the best interests of that community or group to be served, may never be fully resolved. At worst, in several communities, and in several places in post-tsunami Aceh, those purporting to represent the community were often patently not doing so. This sometimes led to a degree of disengagement, misrepresentation, and loss of appropriate outcomes, which were especially wasteful of scarce resources and time. At worst, this often led to corruption, standover tactics (intimidation), both the community and the aid agency being upset, loss of face by all, and compromised outcomes for not only the community but also the donor, the agency, and the government.

Such issues are not easy for the average project management team member to cope with. The *Post-Disaster Rebuild Methodology* (PDRM) (PMI, 2005), a guide published by PMI, provides little focus or guidance on these issues, and most mainstream project management methods related to stakeholders seem to underplay or underestimate this need for stakeholder engagement or how to achieve it. This is particularly surprising given that the definition of project success is generally now agreed to primarily involve stakeholder satisfaction with the project outcomes.

It is very important that the stakeholder engagement process asks which of the most appropriate people/groups are likely to be in alignment with the goals of the project, who may be in conflict, who carries the power or may be better to represent, and who has the greatest need. In this light, there are several processes or methods to engage stakeholders appropriately. Most NGO, UN, EU, Aid Agencies, and governments have manuals and methods for reference to such properties of stakeholders as their needs/credibility, their interest or alignment, their power or conflict with project objectives, their level of commitment, and the communication plans that might most effectively engage them.

The program orientation as a focus for learning also resonated with this Cycle 3. When looking across programs, it becomes even clearer that synergies are missed if there is no cross-project and cross-program learning. In our view, the LogFrame and M&E seem to highlight this more effectively than many traditional project management guides. However, there has been more interest in a balanced scorecard type approach to a more holistic assessment of project performance that includes learning (Norrie & Walker, 2004; Norrie, 2008).

As noted above, two areas of previously identified project management anteced-ents of project management best practices were reinforced through this third action learning cycle—stakeholder engagement and learning across projects and programs. Process and complication overload became another lesson learned from Cycle 3, in that the proposed project management process (in pragmatic terms) needs to be aligned with the sophistication and understanding level of those responsible for de-livering projects. No matter what advantages can accrue from sophisticated program and project management practices, the pragmatic position is that, for the sake of clar-ity and vision acceptance, the quality of project management competence required needs to be matched by supply, so there is much to be done in this respect in terms of "selling the case" for effective program and project management, as has been re-cently attempted (Thomas, Delisle, & Jugdev, 2002; Thomas & Mullaly, 2008).

We will summarize the assessment of Cycle 3 at a point one year through the ongoing VBRRA process. We performed this assessment by examining the lived experience of Paul both as a member of the VBRRA team and as a supervisor of employees from his professional practice (PSA) engaged in the bushfire reconstruc-tion and recovery program. The assessment is based upon process and procedures adopted from daily interactions with members of that group. It presents a detached assessment of Paul's experience in all three action learning cycles to benchmark the evaluation one year after the creation of VBRRA and is presented in Table 4-7 below.

The marginal difference between Cycles 2 and 3 was that the value to outcome impact rose from 3 to 4. This was based upon the experience of using the model de-veloped and refined at Stage 2 with improvements that can be expected when using the approach in a very real and urgent situation where the main project/program outcomes relate to people's lives, rather than just revenue returns from project out-comes, and are far more salient in sustainable project management terms.

It is justifiable to conclude that saturation, from a pragmatic and practical per-spective, had been achieved. The models and approaches, as well as all the findings represented at that point, can be accepted as validated. This represents state-of-the-art until, inevitably, researchers take this work as a point of departure and hope-fully extend its impact. This is indeed the entire purpose of studies like the one reported upon here.

4.5.4 Action Research Cycle 3—Postscript Evaluation

The value of the understanding that was gained through the methods and tech-niques described in this chapter can be confirmed by what happened after the initial engagement of Paul's PSA project management for the bushfire recovery on a "pro bono" basis for the first six months. At the end of that time, the Victorian Bushfire Reconstruction and Recovery Authority were very keen to keep PSA working for

Table 4-7   Criteria Assessment for Action Research Cycle 3

Knowledge, Understanding, and Sense-Making	Workable Practice	Community Internal and External Validation	Value to Outcome Impact
4	4	4	4
Effective sense-making	Effective	Very effective	Effective impact and value

Table 4-8   Criteria Assessment for Action Research Post-Cycle 3

Knowledge, Understanding, and Sense-Making	Workable Practice	Community Internal and External Validation	Value to Outcome Impact
5	4	4	4
Very Effective sense-making	Effective	Very effective	Effective impact and value

them and their respective communities, so they extended that engagement on a commissioned retainer for a further six months, then subsequently for yet another six months.

At the final writing of this book, Paul's practice, and the key people within it, are still engaged in that activity. A salient comment worth recording here is that the Director of Reconstruction recently likened the processes deployed to a "well-oiled machine." This ongoing re-engagement, and the stated satisfaction of the key stakeholder (the authority set up to represent the legitimate interests of bushfire victims), was also a strong form of validation of this work practically and pragmatically applied in the review of both action and research. Our results indicate and, we assert, provide conclusive evidence to support solid understanding and making sense, practice and workability, community engaging internal and external validity, and objective impact on the overall objective in reality. There is clear evidence that the methods outlined here worked effectively in these and earlier environments, and were understandable and workable. Certainly, internal findings were externally validated.

The reviewed impact on the objectives was substantial, so the action research review table representing the post-Cycle 3 situation reflects key value adding of these processes and understandings—both antecedent and project management. The most realistic assessment we can make is presented in Table 4-8.

Time and more comprehensive use and development of the processes advanced will allow realistic long-term evaluation of the workable practice, community internal and external validation, and the value to outcome impact.

4.6 Chapter Summary

This has been a long and dense chapter in terms of content, concepts, evidence, and analysis presented.

The purpose and aim of the chapter was to present an account of how Paul's PhD research supports the research question addressed by this book, namely, how can we best understand the antecedents of project management best practice, and what lessons, if any, from the aid relief project world can enhance this understanding?

The chapter traced a three-cycle action learning approach that rigorously tested a model, which combined lessons learned from the often chaotic or at least complex aid project world of aid/relief projects, together with approaches, suited to the more definable and controllable traditional project management world, that are exemplified by the project management bodies of knowledge (see for example PMI, 2008a). A remarkable level of saturation was achieved in testing for convergence and consistency of findings. The first cycle investigated reflections on over 40 years of documented diary entries on professional practice for a wide range of projects and project types, across a wide range of national and organizational cultures, and on relevant project management literature over several decades. The second cycle involved a highly intensive study of aid projects in distressed regions through an SSM rich-picture approach, which provided salient and valuable insights to allow the reader to share in a vicarious way the experience of being involved in chaotic, or at best complex, aid relief projects in devastated regions of the world. This was followed by action learning Cycle 3, which built upon insights from Cycle 2, and involved the application of lessons learned in testing an approach that melds longstanding (but largely ignored in the traditional project management world) aid project management approaches in a distressed situation in a country where project management practice is well established and well recognized, but which utilized experiences and lessons learned from the less developed world.

The model that emerged out of this cathartic process will be discussed in the next chapter, but it is entirely supported by work that is discussed in this chapter, along with valuable insights from the literature presented in Chapter 2.

5

Findings and Final
Model Summary

5.1 Chapter Introduction

What useful results came out of this research? What is its potential impact?

The final action learning cycle in Chapter 4 described the project management approach as it had evolved into a stable state of acceptance by project management peers, clients, and stakeholders. In this chapter, we will summarize the broader research outcomes arising out of the study. Chapter 4 was a rather lengthy one for readers to quickly absorb, so it is more convenient and logical to summarize outcomes in this shorter chapter. We will address the potential impact of the results in the next chapter, which will close this book and present the overall conclusions.

The contribution made by Paul's thesis in specific terms will be discussed, followed by a chapter summary.

5.2 Summarizing the Contribution of this Book

This book is based on Paul's PhD, with additional insights, an editorial review, and direct input by Derek based on over 20 doctoral theses on related research topics and themes that he has assessed as thesis examiner and supervisor. While the contribution made by this book is a joint one, it should be acknowledged that the research is primarily a product of Paul's PhD thesis work and could not have been completed without the input of an array of project management practitioners and clients whom Paul interviewed during his PhD journey. His CoP was an immensely important support group, as were those colleagues and clients who provided him with data that provided valuable external validation for his 40 years worth of reflective practice. Employees and colleagues of his practice (PSA) provided him with critical and crucial feedback, moral support, and a range of ontological positions on the data.

Paul gathered a mass of data, much of it from quantitative surveys before the actual PhD research. He also gathered a vast body of qualitative data embedded in the rich pictures, while the thousands of feedback emails from his CoP and his own file notes provided support data as well as validation data.

Of great, and often overlooked, significance were the background data gathered in a study such as his. This includes the kind of documented jotting and scribbling of notes that Koskinen (Koskinen & Pihlanto, 2006; Koskinen & Aramo-Immonen, 2008; Koskinen & Mäkinen, 2009) reminds us is so vital for tacit-to-explicit knowledge transfer. It also includes data required for arguably two of the most valuable acts of a professional—*reflecting*, as proposed by Raelin (2001; 2007), and *active sense-making*, as explained by Weick (1988; 1989; 1999; 2001a)—in the service of challenging assumptions and recycling knowledge in a reframed, positive light.

5.2.1. The Philosophical Contribution of this Book

We stated our philosophical position in Chapter 3. Because project management (or at least PMI) aspires to be classed as a profession, some of the characteristics of a profession must be acknowledged and addressed. These include a code of ethical conduct, a quest for knowledge renewal related to the profession concerned, a quest for excellence rather than striving for revenue and material growth, and the capacity and desire to challenge entrenched thinking through reflective practice (Schön, 1983; Wang, 2002; Morris, Crawford, Hodgson, Shepherd, & Thomas, 2006). In our view, part of Paul's contribution can be seen as:

> Support for, and an exemplar of, praxis in the project management domain. Therefore, we suggest that a major contribution made by Paul was to advance the agenda of pragmatism and praxis as a useful guide to undertaking research in project management topics and to demonstrate this contribution through PhD research results.

Praxis, as explained in Chapter 4, Section 3.2.1, is about virtuous performance (love of improved learning, including the maintenance of currency with the relevant literature) and is also associated with dialogue and perception-sharing among peers and between mentor and mentee. Paul's approach to praxis through action research is illustrated in Figure 5-1.

Not only were the *what*, *why* and *how* questions in Figure 5-1 focused on a project management professional research issue, but the research issue itself was studied with a strong, pragmatic, philosophical stance. It leaned toward a positivist paradigm based on a belief that there are project management best practices "out there," yet to be discovered or validated. The ontological stance for the initial stages of the action learning cycle was based on Paul's position as a project manager, and in the second action learning cycle this broadened to the interpreted meaning derived from an aid project, gaining points of view from senior, mid-level, and coal-face practitioners.

The research methods within the action learning cycles included an initial investigation (undertaken as part of action learning Cycle 1) from both the literature and the early surveys that Paul's consultancy had conducted over many years. The second action learning cycle used an SSM research approach, giving way to an interpretive relativist approach with extensive sense-making features where these were pragmatically useful. Far from being a confused mixture of methods and approaches, this approach was entirely consistent with the pragmatic paradigm, in which the epistemological stance argues that validity is about gaining a deeper, more knowledgeable understanding of phenomena, where the outputs from the research are practical and workable, where there is both internal and external validity

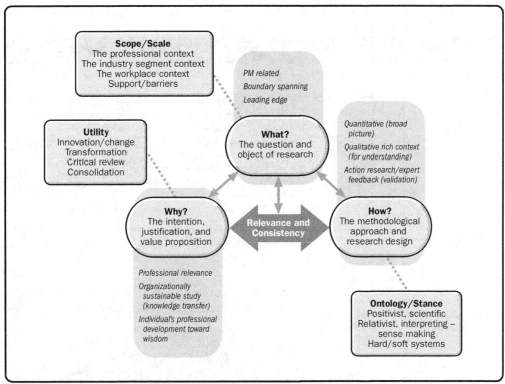

Figure 5-1   Action Research Approach: Source, Walker, Cicmil, Thomas, Anbari and Bredillet (2008b), adapted from Lauriol (2006)

as judged by the professional community identified with the research problem, and where the research outcomes should demonstrate a positive impact on that community (see Table 4-2, Section 4.2).

It would also be fair to suggest that the approach taken through that research elevated Paul's already high level of project management competency from the echelon of competent performer to that of proficient performer/expert (Dreyfus & Dreyfus, 2005) as presented in project management terms by Walker, Cicmil, Thomas, Anbari, and Bredillet (2008), based on the work of Cicmil (Cicmil, 2003; 2006).

We have argued that pragmatism and praxis are relevant to any professional body and community that seek to make a positive difference in the world through the delivery of projects, i.e., realizing beneficial initiatives.

5.2.2. The Project Front-end Focus of this Book

A second contribution that Paul's work has made is to support the growing interest in, and literature addressing (as discussed in Chapter 2, Section 2.4), the importance of project management being intimately engaged at the front end of projects and increasingly involved in program management, where decisions about project selection and prioritization are made. This book's introduction of LogFrame and M&E to the wider traditional project management world community should help other project managers see how valuable those tools and techniques from the aid

Table 5-1   Research and Practice Competency Levels: Adapted from Walker et al. (2008, p. 23)

Level	Experience	Real-Time Action in Context is Driven by
Competent Performer	Amount of experience increases and the number of recognizable learned elements and facts becomes overwhelming.	• Learning from own experience and from others to prioritize elements of the situation • Organizing information by choosing a goal and a plan • Dealing only with a set of key factors relevant to the goal and plan, thus simplifying the task and obtaining improved results • Deliberation about the consequences of using one's own judgment in relation to the given goal and plan (simultaneous subjectivity and objectivity), the relationship of involvement between performer and environment • The model of analytical, proficient performer: Elements-rules-goals-plans-decision • Ability to think on one's feet (confidence, reflection, choice of action, and risk taking)
Proficient Performer	Away from cognitivist, analytical rationality (rules, principles, and universal solutions), toward perceiving situations rapidly, intuitively, holistically, visually, bodily, relationally.	• The awareness of interpretation and judgment involved in such decision making, rather than logical information processing and analytical problem-solving only • Understanding of the situation on the basis of prior actions and experience, acts as deeply "involved-in-the-world" manager/performer who already knows • Reflective understanding and participation in power relations
Expert or Virtuoso		• Reflective learning; simultaneous thinking and doing • Intuitive, synchronous understanding of the situation with an overarching participative critical reflection of the self and the group • The thought, body, knowledge, and action are inseparable, are simultaneously forming and are being formed by one another • Understanding that power relating is an intrinsic part of inter-subjective relating, and is always there • Considerations for the present and deliberations about the future

project world are and how they may be effectively adapted or co-opted. Figure 5-2 illustrates the way that programs and project cycles can be visualized.

Figure 5-2 illustrates the *what, why,* and *how* questions illustrated in Figure 5-1 in a way that links action learning to program and project management. Koskinen (Koskinen, Pihlanto, & Vanharanta, 2003; Koskinen, 2010) has argued that projects can be seen as learning factories, and as places where project knowledge is created, further developed, shared, and used. Paul's Figure 5-2 helps us see how that knowledge work occurs and how it can provide pragmatic outputs and outcomes.

The situation analysis questions posed by Paul's Figure 5-2 provided a contribution to the way that this critical front-end activity was addressed.

Questions posed at this step include:

• What are the intended objectives or goals of the overall intervention, and how may their impacts be assessed?
• What is the real situation framing this intended intervention? (What is the environment within which this situation is to be resolved? What key groups will be involved here? What are their key values/criteria for success? What are the key outcomes in focus here, and are they feasible and agreed?)

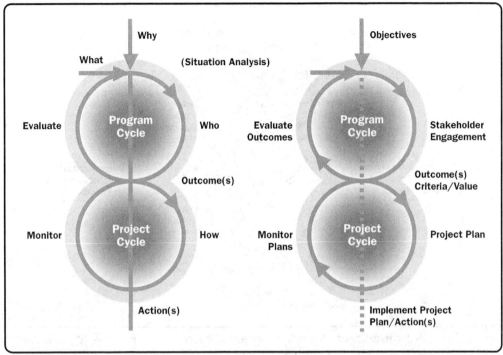

Figure 5-2   Program to Project Linkage Viewed as an Action Learning Cycle

- Why do this? Does this fit within the organization's overall vision/mission/ values/key criteria/authentic leadership/competence?
- Who are the key stakeholders? Which of them will be critical, aligned, committed, driving, and conflicting, and are their values addressed in the outcomes to be resolved?
- How can key program outcomes be resolved and achieved *with* the key stakeholders, and are they feasible and supportable? How can the project deliverables/outputs/inputs/activities deliver the necessary value to the outcomes to enable the overall objectives/impact? (Do they align with the organization's criteria for success?)

Outcomes to appropriate values can be resolved and agreed upon, and through these steps a project plan to deliver the program can be developed. The two-cycle process can then be used to regularly review project management progress. Also, the program cycle can be used on a less regular basis to evaluate the delivery of outcomes and their value to, and impact on, the overall objective to address real problems in the real situation, with due respect for the values and the stakeholder environment.

The project management approach here may be similar to that traditionally undertaken in the past, but now it has greater identification of the outcomes and deliverables and, in turn, of the key value identification part of selecting the best projects/outcomes/objectives.

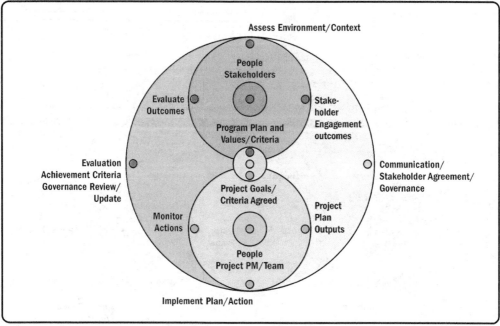

Figure 5-3   Synthesis of Project Program Organization Process in Balance of Nature in an Eastern Yin-Yang Graphic Format

The earlier discussion of the LogFrame approach (see Section 2.6, Figure 2-3 and Table 2-4) provides rich-picture examples of the typically messy situations that project management practitioners find themselves in for aid relief projects. They can then adapt and use lessons learned from those situations to better link program and project management cycles. While program management standards exist (PMI, 2006b), they are formative and in the early stages of their development. Paul's work has helped to provide real-life examples for the project management community to consider and adapt.

His color-coded synthesized project management best practices model, illustrated in Figure 4-14, is reproduced here as Figure 5-3. The color coding in particular adds clarity to the linking of stakeholders and processes. This is particularly salient at the front end in deciding upon an initiative through understanding the purpose to be served and by M&E based on coherent and consistent LogFrame objectives. The yin-yang model provides balance, as indicated below:

5.2.3   The Research Methods Focus
Another useful contribution made to the development of a research method arose out of the pragmatic research paradigm. Figure 5-4 illustrates this model.

The research outcomes were assessed against the pragmatic criteria: increasing knowledge and understanding, and thus making sense; being practical and workable; being internally and externally acceptable and validated by the community sharing project management values; and having an objective impact.

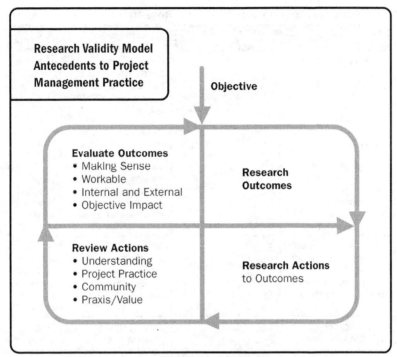

Figure 5-4   Research Validity Model

An example from the third action research cycle illustrates how this model can be presented in practice and was provided in Table 4-2 in Section 4.2. This was further extended in Paul's thesis to contribute a clearer and fuller explanation of the levels of results obtained in terms of the pragmatic paradigm's validation criteria. An example of the final stage of the action learning cycles is presented in Table 4-7, with the explanation of the ratings clearly provided in Table 5-2.

Paul also mapped convergence in an innovative way across the three research cycles in his thesis, as illustrated in Figure 5-5.

Paul has therefore given us, through his thesis, a model that other researchers may choose to follow to measure the level of saturation of findings from each successive action learning cycle. Often researchers are bewildered by the term "saturation" and wonder what it means in a practical and pragmatic sense. The approach of devising a monitoring and assessment model to not only measure the degree of convergence, but to also do it in a transparent way, provides researchers with a general tool to work with when they adopt a pragmatic paradigm. These tools are useful for visualizing, and therefore demonstrating, convergence and saturation of the action learning cycle results. This novel approach may be adapted and used by other researchers.

5.2.4   Contribution to Application of SSM

The final methodological contribution that we wish to draw to the attention of readers is the innovations that Paul's thesis provides for researchers who may be considering using SSM as a research approach.

Table 5-2   Summary Evaluation of Action Research Learning Cycle 3

Criteria	Evaluation	Relative Weighting	Knowledge	Understanding
Making Sense	While already validated, it was valuable to further test understanding over an extended range of programs and projects and in a different environment from that of the preceding research	**4.3** Proved to be more extensive and effective than foreseen	Knowledge mostly consolidated in Cycle 2, but further validated and improved upon in this final cycle	Understanding greatly improved upon in this final and extended research cycle
Workable	While already validated, it was very valuable to a seasoned practitioner to apply over a further extended range and in a more direct context	**4** All really worked through and resolved	Significant gain in validation and knowledge in the extending of internal learning from one environment to the next	Significantly improved validation and understanding in applying, testing, and improving models in practice over an extended period of time and place
Internal & External	It was resolved and taken to a great extent in communities and practice, in further contexts, and at a range of levels and points of view	**4** All really worked through and resolved	Significant gain in validation and knowledge in the extending of internal learning from one environment to the next	Significantly improved validation and understanding in applying, testing, and improving models in practice over an extended period of time and place
Objective Impact	This proved to generate significant impact and understanding. The challenge now is how to carry it forward to realize the overall impact it could have in the environment and several contexts where it can be of obvious value, specifically and globally	**3.6** Solid impact, but there is still a lot for it to be taken to and research to build on	Validating knowledge by the practice outcomes and findings, and improvements and validation enabled through the extended application, testing, and realization of proven models in practice and acceptance	Real understanding gained by key project people at a range of levels and practice The objectives were achieved better than everyone expected or even thought possible, and the importance of the simply, robustly effective together with the authentic leadership proved very valuable and will endure

Section 3.3.2 discussed and explained the seven SSM steps, and in Section 4.4.2, in which the second action learning cycle used SSM as its core, the research approach placed particular emphasis on rich pictures as a useful way to make explicit many examples of tacit knowledge where emotion and feelings are so important for genuine understanding of a messy situation under study.

Paul introduced three important innovations in the use of SSM, which were illustrated in subsection 4.4.2.1 in the examples describing rich pictures. The rich pictures presented in Figures 4.5 to 4.8 provide graphic and highly informative representations of the messy situations encountered from several ontological stances, and they are innovative from several perspectives.

First, Paul developed a color-coding system that accentuated emotions and made them more vivid. Figure 4-9 in subsection 4.4.2.1 provided an explanation of the logic behind his approach. Second, he depicted themes in ellipses that summed up groups of important data, as explained in Figure 4-10. Third, he was able to synthesize these themes into a summative rich picture of key concepts, using the rich picture themes and stories as data that could paint a broader picture of the lived

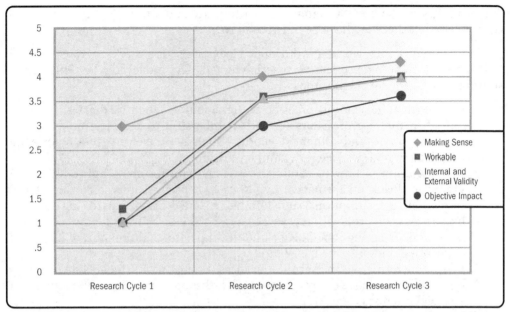

Figure 5-5   Mapping Convergence by Research Validity

realities of those experiencing the analyzed messy situations. We suggest that this contribution to tools for sense-making is significant.

5.2.5 Contribution to Reflective Practice

In subsection 5.2.1 above, we stressed the importance of Paul's journey of reflective practice to his PhD. This thesis may provide a useful example of how reflective practice can be enacted in such a way that it moves from thinking about action to thinking in action. Further, by following a pragmatic action learning approach, he has been able to capitalize on past experience, as documented through reflective journals, and has incorporated these into a justified research design leading to the action learning cycles and to the channeling of this work into a PhD thesis.

This kind of doctoral-level thesis, in which a reflective practitioner's journey of knowledge exploration is used as a basis for rigorous research, has been done before; recently, Derek supervised another such journey (Arroyo, 2009), resulting in a successful doctorate, and he has also examined another doctoral thesis (Sense, 2005) that could be seen as having been undertaken by a reflective practitioner. Thus, we can see the emergence of a trend, a slowly evolving channel, by which reflective practitioners can use a doctoral study as a focus for their reflection and thereby contribute both to their discipline and to their personal practice.

We feel that Paul's PhD work, and this book, contribute to reflective practice in two ways. First, they provide a map or approach that proved viable for the dual purpose of advancing project management practice and Paul's professional development in a way that would not otherwise have been possible had it been restricted to, for example, a mentoring or coaching situation. The rigor of a PhD forced an innovative adaptation of research methods, greater depth in thinking about and justifying the assumptions that Paul had as a seasoned practitioner, and his engagement in a far deeper review of the project management literature and a range of other literature than he would otherwise have been exposed to.

In summary, this work had an added advantage for any concrete research findings by developing a reflective practice model. The model for this PhD can be summarized in the following steps:

1. Long-term reflection on practice using resources such as diaries (often required in many professions for full membership to a professional association), file notes, and company records—such as project progress reports and post-project reviews (see for example Williams, 2007).

2. Consideration of how to establish a mechanism for challenging ideas, providing feedback on formative hypotheses or propositions, creating friction to challenge assumptions, and forcing reasoned argument to justify ideas, hypotheses, or propositions; these may be done through being coached or mentored, engaging in a CoP, or undertaking a formal program of high level conceptual and practice-based study.

3. Presenting formative and summative ideas through professional body meetings, symposia, conferences, or other forms of workshops, or through interaction with a special interest group (SIG).

4. Publishing results to enable others to gain insights from the work; relevant documentation includes academic papers, theses, blogs, or other media that expose the work to scrutiny and adaptation by others.

5.2.6 Contribution to Project Management Theory—The Antecedents of Project Management Best Practice

This subsection will summarize Paul's findings related to the antecedents of project management best practice. This has been reserved until now not because it is the least important result of his PhD work, but rather because it provides a summative closure to this work. The main research outcomes and conclusions to Paul's work are summarized as follows.

Readers can refer to Figure 5-6 as an enduring model that summarizes project management best practice. The clustered practices set out therein will not be new to many experienced project managers, and it would be fair to ask whether there is anything new about this contribution. Our response is that many of these practices reaffirm previously held and published beliefs about best practice, but as the rethinking project management movement pointed out some five years ago, the project management profession has assumed much that has not been tested by empirical evidence.

This study of Paul's did precisely that, through considerable survey work in action learning Cycle 1 (which may satisfy those who have charged project management research with not being objective enough in finding meta-data to support or refute so-called success factors). Paul undertook extensive and deep research work through the SSM study to uncover the lived experience of project management team members in highly challenging and complex contexts. This may satisfy those critics who claim that deterministic and instrumental research fails to uncover the fine-grained data to be found in qualitative research using interpretivist or critical realist approaches to data analysis. Finally, he validated his findings through action

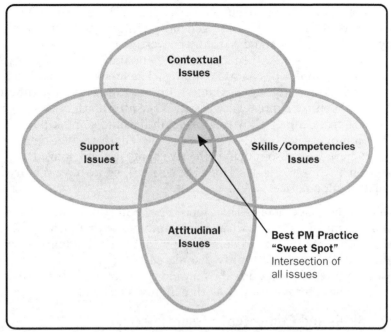

Figure 5-6   Understanding of Issues Influencing Project Management Best Practice

learning Cycle 3, in which an in vivo experiment was effectively carried out to implement the project management best practices that we will present. This should satisfy critics who claim that pragmatic justification by reflective practitioners who are experts in their field is needed to shed light on the strengths and limitations of theories and vaunted best practice.

We addressed the "antecedents" of project management best practice in Chapter 1, Section 1.3, citing the Oxford Dictionary's definition of "a thing or event that existed logically or logically precedes another" (Pearsall & Hanks, 2001, p. 69). We will now look at w*hat things must happen and be in place* before the phenomenon of project management best practice can be realized. There are four issue groups at play relating to project management practice, as illustrated in Figure 5-6—contextual, skills and competencies, support (structural), and attitudinal.

Each of these issues will now be addressed.

5.2.6.1 Contextual Issues

The results from each of the research cycles emerged from different contextual situations, and along with them came an assumed paradigm about what project management is.

In Cycle 1, which was centered on Paul's personal project management practice and his professional practicing firm (PSA), the guiding paradigm was that project management is mainly associated with "earth"-type projects (see Chapter 2, Section 2.2), though his experience did include some projects that could be classified as "water," "fire," and even "air"-type projects. Most uncertainties faced in engineering projects, as earlier discussed in Section 2.7.1, using the Cynefyn framework (Snowden & Boone, 2007), were generally either simple or complicated domains in which the context and environment were generally somewhat ordered. In Cycle 2, the rich pictures described an environment and context of general unorder or disorder within complex or chaotic domains. The lessons learned from Cycles 1 and 2 were absorbed in preparing for Cycle 3, mitigating against the inherent chaos surrounding the bushfire aid recovery effort in the aftermath of the tragedy by applying some structure, albeit allowing for flexibility and some kind of "muddling through" by improvisation, as discussed at some length in Section 2.7.1. Cycle 3 was deemed to have been a sound and effective approach and, judged one year after the intervention by the criteria described in Section 4.5.3, to have achieved "better" project management practice.

The point to be made here is that applying the narrow strategy of a quite detailed plan-and-control project management paradigm with a major task focus may be perfectly suitable for an ordered domain (environmental context). Also, it is good practice within unordered and highly disordered contexts to apply a project management paradigm of setting a broad overarching vision and objectives, and to be highly adaptive and improvisational, with a highly relational focus.

5.2.6.2 Skills and Competency Issues

The proficient performer or expert virtuoso knows when to switch leadership styles, as discussed in Section 2.7.3, based on cultural complexity such as that discussed in Section 2.7.2, and how to deal with a situation and lead in an authentic manner. While this leads us into skills and competencies issues, it highlights their interaction with context.

In Chapter 2, Section 2.7.3, we discussed leadership and leadership styles. Müller and Turner's (2007) summary of project management success and project manager leadership style provides a good guide for best practice:

> Managers of project managers need to be aware that different leadership styles exhibited by the project manager are appropriate on different types of projects. Managers need to be aware of the needs of projects in their organization, develop individuals for the pool of available projects. (p. 31)

This leads Müller and Turner (Turner & Müller, 2005; Turner et al., 2009) to one general precept for project management best practice—project managers need intellectual intelligence (IQ), project managerial intelligence (MQ), and emotional intelligence (EQ). Our Action Learning Cycle 2 findings, in particular, suggest that in the unordered or disordered contexts in Cynefin Framework terms (Snowden & Boone, 2007), greater and more sophisticated levels of stakeholder engagement are necessary to better make sense of, and understand, any environment and context. This demands higher levels of EQ. We argue that one antecedent of project management best practice is signaled by project teams—and, in particular, a project team leader—having a strong capacity to empathize with others and very high sense-making skills. This should be seen as essential for dealing with project front-end activities such as development and communication of a strong project vision, and how the project fits into a coherent program of projects. As stated in Section 2.7, this is associated with authentic leadership skills.

5.2.6.3 Support Issues

The ability of project management practitioners to visualize the big picture, so that they can motivate others to effectively deliver projects, needs to be complemented by the necessary organizational and structural support mechanisms to allow good leadership to flourish and not be inhibited. Figure 2-3 in subsection 2.6.2 illustrated this in terms of project governance, and in Section 2.3 it was noted that top management support, strong and involved sponsorship, and other factors and processes related to project governance emerged as clear indicators of sound, and in fact best, project management practice.

Therefore, a further antecedent of project management best practice would appear to be demonstrated strong support systems for the project manager, ones that help them not only to carry out the more traditional project management practices such as planning, monitoring, and controlling progress on projects, but also to provide empowerment and political and organizational support, so that internal as well as external stakeholder engagement can be effective.

5.2.6.4 Attitudinal Issues

This aspect of the antecedents of project management best practice became much clearer during the reflection stages of each of the three action learning cycles. As Paul moved forward using the action learning cycle approach based on a pragmatic paradigm of value fixed at the core of best practice, it became obvious that project management best practice was inextricably bound up with a thirst for knowledge—poetically, we put this as drinking from the well of knowledge. Indeed the water analogy is highly relevant here. The origin of the word *argument* lies in the word *agua* or water (i.e., clear, pure water). It implies that the purpose of an argument is to take the impure (water) and, through a purposeful process of refinement, convert it into the pure (water). The process of refining an argument involves challenging assumptions and is based on finding knowledge gaps, falsehoods, and inaccuracies in order to identify and eradicate impurity so that the end result is pristine and wholly adapted to its purpose.

Action learning is a process of argument, and the steps are essentially argumentative. The reflection is a process of challenging assumptions and searching for meaningful ways to see a situation. The plan and act parts of the action learning cycle are not undertaken in haste; rather, they are experimental and in themselves reflective. In Section 3.3.3, we stressed that action learning should have a dual action *and* learning purpose. The evaluation and validation phases are parts of the purification process or argument. The pragmatic approach is also important as an attitudinal trait that suggests best practice. Evaluation criteria, as discussed in Chapter 2, Section 2.6.1, should be relevant, effective, efficient, and sustainable and have positive impact. These are pragmatic criteria. Pragmatic epistemology, the way that validity is seen by pragmatists and the way that we present it in Table 4-2 (Chapter 4, Section 4.2), makes several demands. "Proof" and "evidence" should increase knowledge and understanding about the thing to be proved, the approach to seeking them should be practical and workable, the community with the relevant authority and credibility should deem the approach to be internally and externally valid, and the result should lead to fulfilling a valid objective.

Thus, to ensure likely project management best practice, the team delivering a project must therefore be composed of pragmatic reflective practitioners who value praxis as described earlier in Chapter 3, Section 3.3.3.

5.2.6.5 Issues Summary

In summarizing subsection 5.2.6, we suggest that, in meta-analysis terms, project management best practice are likely to be present at the "sweet spot" indicated in Figure 5-6. This is where understanding of contextual issues intersects with having sufficient organizational support, skills, and competencies, along with an attitude that supports reflective practice and praxis to continually keep project management best practice alive through testing, challenge, and argument—with the pragmatic aim of continuous improvement, i.e., striving for excellence.

Table 5-3   Summarized Examples of Project Management Best Practice Antecedent Action Required

Antecedent Issue	Summarized example of how antecedents to project management best practice may be actioned — Through >>>
Contextual, (i.e., environment, culture, power balance)	• Summarizing, in a simple but effective universal framework, contextually appropriate project methods for application in any environment. • Providing a significantly improved understanding of the necessary project management work needed at the front end of projects in general. • Identifying the necessary effective project management practices in any environment and how they may work in all ranges of projects. • Acknowledging core value and synergies in each of the project management body of knowledge methods employed around the world for traditional project management work, and knowing what simple, robust, and effective methods and elements to apply in particular circumstances and contexts.
Skills and Competencies, (i.e., hard skills, soft skills, abilities)	• Facilitating an improvement in the way projects are understood, approached, planned, and managed. • Gaining significant knowledge – at personal, group, and organizational community of practice levels – of what constitutes project management practice. • Gaining a good understanding of project management best practice at community of practice and professional project manager levels. • Significantly improving understanding and applying validation and testing of how to improve models in practice (organizational learning).
Support, (i.e., frameworks, templates, sponsorship, championing, resources)	• Providing a sound and demonstrated example of project management process improvement and how, perhaps through an action learning approach, people close to these projects can develop their own self-help approaches, which can be specifically deployed to bridge the gaps in project management practice that they encounter and identify. • Providing a template of an approach that others in a similar predicament can follow to identify and address gaps or absences in project management best practice. • Achieving a good understanding of project management best practices through facilitating the development of a diverse but relevant set of communities of practice. • Gaining significant validation and knowledge of how to extend internal learning from one environment to the next. • Validating knowledge by the practice outcomes, findings, and improvements enabled through the extended application, testing, and acceptance of proven models in practice.
Attitudes, (i.e., leadership, followership, team élan, motivation, learning, praxis)	• Focusing, simplifying, and clarifying action research and project management process in everyday project practice. • Realizing the benefit of praxis to everyday and community projects and project management in general. • Having a propensity for developing emotional intelligence. • Having an open mind and seeking to challenge current approaches in order to make improvements. • Having integrity and the drive to engage in continuous improvement.

Next we can ask how the antecedents of project management best practice may be translated into action; that is, what needs to be done?

This categorization of the antecedents of project management best practice can be presented in a form (Table 5-3) that presents examples of what action may trigger that best practice, so that the "what needs to be done?" question is addressed.

5.2.7 Contribution to Project Management Research

Table 5-4 identifies the rethinking project management agenda and how this research contributes to that initiative. This final subsection concludes our discussion.

We purposely linked this last subsection to Section 2.5 in Chapter 2 and the work undertaken by the "rethinking project management" group of academics and practitioners. We did so because their seminal paper (Winter et al., 2006) provides a table in which five directions for research were offered. We stated earlier that we believed we had effectively addressed these directions though this research. It seems appropriate therefore for us to present project management best practices in a format, which is congruent to those five research directions.

Table 5-4   Examples of the Research into the Antecedents to Project Management Best Practices Linking to the Rethinking Project Management Initiative

Research Direction	Identified Antecedents to Project Management Best Practice—Summarized from Figure 4-13 Key Concepts	Research is Justification in Terms of: Evaluation, Criteria, and Benefit
Direction 1 – Theory ABOUT practice **Lifecycle theories to complexity theories** *From* the life cycle models of projects and project management as the dominant model of projects and project management *to* the development of new models and theories, which recognize and illuminate the complexity of projects and project management *From* often unexamined assumptions of the life cycle model as the "actual" project management terrain *to* new models and theories, which are explicitly presented as only *partial* theories of the complex "reality"	A need for more focus on the front end of projects, for defining purpose (goals), expected outcomes, what outputs are needed to deliver those outcomes, what activities are therefore required, and what assumptions underlie them. Rapid assessment of environment, context, and needs.	**Evaluation Criteria**–Efficiency, Relevance **Benefit**–Greater focus on getting the project objectives and vision well understood at the front end of projects. Getting outputs and outcomes better understood and clarifying assumptions made. **Impact**–Better statement of a project's purpose and place within a program and gaining a wider, more holistic view of project management, approaches, tools, and techniques (from other parts of the project management world and from general management) that may be usefully applied.

Table 5-4   Examples of the Research into the Antecedents to Project Management Best Practices Linking to the Rethinking Project Management Initiative *(continued)*

Research Direction	Identified Antecedents to Project Management Best Practice—Summarized from Figure 4-13 Key Concepts	Research is Justification in Terms of: Evaluation, Criteria, and Benefit
Direction 2–Theory FOR practice Instrumental process to social processes *From* projects as instrumental processes composed of linear task sequences using highly codified knowledge, procedures, and techniques, and projects as temporary, apolitical production processes *to* projects as social processes with interaction among people, illuminating the flux of events and human interaction within a complex array of social agenda, practices, stakeholder relations, politics and power	Engaging stakeholders and defining outcomes as a critical project front-end activity and empathizing with the cultural norms and perspectives, values, and therefore perspectives of what project success means.	**Evaluation Criteria**–Relevance, Sustainability, Effectiveness **Benefit**–By focusing on key stakeholders' requirements whose needs prompted the project in the first place, their expectations can be better gauged and managed, and feedback about their fulfillment through the project can be better communicated. **Impact**–More informed key stakeholders who interact more constructively with the project delivery team, less disruption through unanticipated resistance, more long-term support.
Direction 3–Theory FOR practice Product creation to value creation *From* concepts and methodologies, which focus on product criteria and narrow conceptualizations at the project's start *to* concepts and frameworks that focus on value generation as the prime project focus	Continued evaluation of project outputs as maintaining expected delivery of program outcomes. Understanding the continuous relevance and sustainability of a project within a program. Returning to rapid assessment, where and when context, environment, or needs change the original purpose to achieve a sustainable outcome.	**Evaluation Criteria**–Relevance, Sustainability, Effectiveness, Impact **Benefit**–By closely evaluating the program and the project's place in that program, the relevance and worth of the project can be better understood. The project can be supported and better maintained with resources, if viable. If not viable, the project can then be terminated and scarce resources redeployed rather than be wasted if the project ceases to be necessary or has failed to add value to the program objectives. Clarity of vision and objectives are maintained through evaluation. Better assessment tools avoid misuse of scarce resources. **Impact**–Requires keen political knowledge if a project is to be shelved or closed down, to be able to persuade key stakeholders of the justification and rationale for such decisions.

Table 5-4   Examples of the Research into the Antecedents to Project Management Best Practices Linking to the Rethinking Project Management Initiative *(continued)*

Research Direction	Identified Antecedents to Project Management Best Practice—Summarized from Figure 4-13 Key Concepts	Research is Justification in Terms of: Evaluation, Criteria, and Benefit
Direction 4–Theory FOR practice **Narrow conceptualization of projects to broader conceptualization of projects** *From* concepts and approaches, which are based on the narrow conceptualization that projects start from "given" at the start *to* concepts and approaches, which facilitate broader and ongoing conceptualization of projects as being multidisciplinary—having multiple purposes, networks of contributors and membership—and that renegotiation of roles and functions is contestable	Planning and monitoring project progress toward value generation by taking a value chain approach to link the beneficiaries of a project or program initiative to the project output and outcome. The discovery of the usefulness of LogFrame and M&E is salient to this research aims. Risks being seen as socially constructed phenomena needing identification *and* engagement from stakeholders.	**Evaluation Criteria**–Relevance, Effectiveness, Efficiency **Benefit**–The LogFrame and M&E approaches provide the high level assurance of staying relevant. The actual project delivery stage may need times of intense focus using traditional project management tools and techniques. This research highlighted the yin and yang of project and program interaction and synergy. **Impact**–Requires an ability to manage the complementarities of taking a broad helicopter view while also being focused on details. Requires a *bricoleur* approach to sense-making and action.
Direction 5–Theory IN practice **From practitioners as trained technicians to practitioners as reflective practitioners** *From* an emphasis on training, which produces practitioners who follow prescriptive procedures and techniques *to* an emphasis on learning and development, which facilitates reflection, praxis, and pragmatic action	While Figure 4-13 does not identify reflective learning, praxis, and organizational learning, it does imply this through the evaluate, reflect, and understand emphases.	**Evaluation Criteria**–Relevance, Effectiveness, Sustainability **Benefit**–This work has a significant benefit through praxis that knowledge will flow more easily and be less slick. Individuals benefit from being reflective, and through exchanging ideas, groups communities and organizations gain longer term benefit. **Impact**–Requires much effort to build in learning and knowledge transfer as a recognized project outcome and project to program outcome.

The purpose of Table 5-4 was to illustrate how Paul's work and this book should be viewed as contributors to research as well as practice, and to advocate the need to seek pragmatic results and outcomes.

5.3 Chapter Summary

This chapter summarized the findings and contributions of Paul's PhD thesis, which are reported on in this book. The actual summary unfolded under a series of subheadings.

We showed how Paul's work and this book provide a number of contributions to the project management profession and to project management academic aspirations. The contributions were philosophical, a focus on the front end of projects, a focus on the research methods adopted by this work, contributions to the way that SSM may be applied, contributions to reflective practice, and, finally, not just identifying the antecedents of project management best practice, but providing some ways of understanding them and seeing how they may be triggered in organizations.

We argue that this contribution extends and enhances the work undertaken under the rethinking project management banner (Winter & Smith, 2006; Winter et al., 2006), which has been an important inspiration for the work undertaken by Paul for his PhD, and has also been summarized in this book.

The contribution can be seen as having two beneficiaries—project management practice and research about project management practice.

The next chapter will wrap up the book with a short conclusion and a discussion of implications for project management practice.

6

Conclusions

6.1 Chapter Introduction

What is the potential impact of this research? How can it be useful to the project management profession?

This chapter will conclude the book by answering these practical and pragmatic questions and it is structured as follows. The next section specifically answers the above questions. This is followed by a section that concludes the book and shows how it fulfilled the aims and objectives set out in Chapter 1. A short section then identifies further research and practice initiatives that could flow from this work. A chapter summary finalizes the book.

6.2 Implications of the Research Reported on in the Book

From a pragmatic perspective, we have consistently undertaken our research and writing to enable the work to be useful to two communities—project management practitioners and project management scholars, but we do acknowledge and recognize a subset of both groups that could be called "pracademics." They are reflective practitioners who, through their praxis, consider each experience as a learning opportunity and have affective commitment toward the *plan > act > observe > reflect* cycle. These "pracademics" may be primarily positioned in academia or practice and usually work within both types of organizations, often simultaneously.

The subsections of this section will first discuss the implications for practitioners and how this work may impact them and their stakeholders. Following that, we discuss the impact of the research and its implications for project management scholarship.

6.2.1 Impact and Implications for Project Management Practice

Four main impacts and implications are summarized in Figure 6-1 below.

6.2.1.1 Thinking about the Program/Project Interface

The first implication of the impact of the findings to practice is thinking about the roles of projects within programs. This could be liberating for project management practice. The recent focus on project management research and practice development has been centered on strategy, with the explicit aim of projects being firmly seen as delivery vehicles of outputs which, when combined with other projects, deliver valuable outcomes and benefits. Paul's work has reinforced that by establishing a clearer link between projects and programs, using tools that are shown to work to that end. The LogFrame and the M&E tools, or a variant of them, provide clear

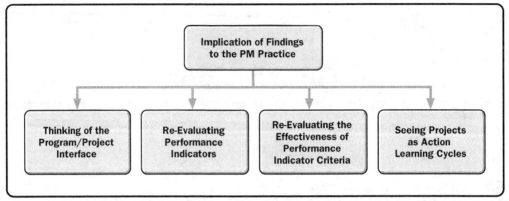

Figure 6-1   High Level Summary of Research Implications to Project Management Practice

ways in which projects can be mapped and integrated into programs. Figure 4-14 in Section 4.4.2.3 (reproduced in Section 5.2.2, Figure 5-3) illustrates the yin and yang synergy of program objectives being met by project activities. Figure 4-15 in Section 4.4.3 provides a clear map of a project program organization cycle, showing a 12-key factor process. This provides immediate tools to define roles and responsibilities.

This research allowed tools and techniques to be tested and refined through the VBRRA third action learning cycle. Impact and usefulness are summarized in Table 6-1.

These are now used as standard and indispensable project management tools for program management in the VBRRA program of projects. It will be interesting to see how this may affect other post-disaster programs of projects, as well as more traditional project management practices.

6.2.1.2   Re-evaluating Performance Indicators

We saw in Section 2.3 that project management performance success and project performance success have been recognized as different. The iron triangle of time/cost/fitness for purpose has been expanded to be more focused on stakeholder engagement and notions of how to best monitor and evaluate projects. This leads to evaluation criteria from M&E being seen as relevant, as explained in Section 2.6.1. The focus on evaluation performance indicators such as *relevance, efficiency, effectiveness, impact,* and *sustainability* provides a paradigm shift in how performance indicators are viewed. Answers to the impact questions are presented in Table 6-2.

Table 6-1   Impact and Usefulness of Rethinking Program to Project Interface

What is the potential impact of this research?	Projects are more clearly framed within a program's intended benefits outcome delivery.
How can it be useful to the project management profession?	Better mapping and the adaptation of aid project world tools, techniques, and approaches provide better vision definition, scoping mechanisms, and stakeholder engagement.

Table 6-2   Impact and Usefulness of Re-evaluating Performance Indicators

What is the potential impact of this research?	Project performance indicator mapping being more clearly seen as needed to contribute to program success in terms of intended benefits to be delivered.
How can it be useful to the project management profession?	Better mapping of how a project performs in terms of being relevant and effectively and efficiently managed, so that outputs are sustainable and produce positive impact to a program – leading to a more holistic view of project and project management success.

The re-evaluation extends the performance indicator concept to another level. Relevance, impact, and sustainability are aligned with a specific project's output performance indicators as being one of a series of coherently linked complementary project output performance indicators, so that the outcome produces the desired positive impact on the benefit to be delivered. Seen in this way, the individual project then needs to be relevant to the program context, aims, and vision, as well as producing a result, or an output, that contributes in a sustainable way to the program aim. The "iron triangle" project management success indicators are parts of the efficiency evaluation performance indicator, so they are not abandoned or lost, but rather extended by this perspective. Table 2-5 (in Section 2.6.2) presented the performance criteria, including economic performance indicators, that may be considered part of being efficient in terms of the cost of assessment versus the benefit of the value of information obtained. Similarly, timely and sensitive performance criteria may be considered part of being effective, in terms of optimizing the value of the M&E effort.

6.2.1.3   Re-evaluating the Effectiveness of Performance Indicator Criteria
This work reinforced the primacy of relevance. Project performance needs to be relevant and purposeful to serve the aims and objectives of the program and project and deliver the expected benefit. Accepting the pragmatic paradigm thus leads to a need for the M&E effort to be both valuable and value-adding. Therefore, any measures used to monitor and evaluate should follow the criteria used in Table 4-2 in Section 4.2. In Section 3.4, we stated that evaluation criteria should facilitate *knowledge and understanding/sense-making*, be *practical and workable*, demonstrate *community internal/external validity*, and produce an *objective impact* on the monitoring exercise.

Monitoring activities, subproject strings of related activities, or entire projects should lead to improved performance. Traditionally, the monitoring process in project management leads to action being taken with the aim of maintaining progress to plan, or influencing how an unrealistic plan can be reshaped to be more practical. However, large leakages of lessons learned, knowledge, and cause-and-effect insights occur. Sometimes the performance measures used do not measure what is important to the stakeholders who could benefit from the information and knowledge.

This contribution to project performance adds to that framework so that a performance management system is not only practical and workable, but also acceptable to the community in a best position to judge performance. That is, it should be internally and externally valid while having an internal logic that explains the purpose of the performance criteria concerned and promotes better understanding of cause-and-effect links. While traditional project management time management

Table 6-3   Impact and Usefulness of Re-evaluating Activity Effectiveness Criteria

What is the potential impact of this research?	Performance criteria, being less exception-management driven, become more transformational in their outcome – performance measurement and management become more clearly a part of continuous improvement and the learning cycle.
How can it be useful to the project management profession?	Using the five criteria noted in bold above could transform performance measurement from using lagging indicators to these leading indicators. For example, instead of measuring planning quality in terms of activity time performance success, it might be measured by how it clarifies understanding about component and system integration and how it affects the expected program outcome.

tools such as bar charts and critical path analysis are useful for more technically oriented team members, they may not be understandable or apparently valid to other stakeholders, who may more easily comprehend the same message when it is transformed into simulation graphics, or trust and believe it to be valid when it is in metaphorical media and communication channels with which they are familiar.

6.2.1.4   Seeing Projects as Action Learning Cycles

Once Paul started to see projects in an action learning cycle of *plan > do > observe > reflect*, he was able to see how the missing link of learning within and between projects could be remedied. The point of departure for this work was seeing project management as an action learning process in which knowledge becomes a key asset and, therefore, of key strategic competitive advantage. A closer focus on the learning was gained from the project management experience on each project as a result of this paradigm shift. This has profound potential impact on what constitutes success. It could, for example, lead to these probing questions about a project:

- What do we now know more about with regard to stakeholder characteristics, desires, potential influence, and preferred engagement strategies?
- What technical, commercial, and relationship knowledge "owned" by project team member X could be of value to team member Y on project A, or to team member Z on project B, etc.?
- What were the principal forces and dynamics in play on project L that led to action M resulting in outcome N?

There are many such questions that could be illustrated here to highlight how traditional project management often fails to manage knowledge within project boundaries or across projects. These questions serve to illustrate a massive gap in value realization in project management, and remedying this can be prompted by changing the paradigm from projects as delivering outputs toward realization of a tangible objective, to one where projects are additionally seen as valuable experimental playgrounds where valuable knowledge is created and individual people and groups involved can increase their absorptive capacity and reduce the stickiness of knowledge transfer.

Two terms used in this context need clarifying. *Knowledge stickiness* is the perceived difficulty of knowledge being transferred between people. Szulanski (1996) identified "a barren context" as being one of a number of identified factors that explain knowledge stickiness. A barren context is one that does not encourage

Table 6-4   Impact and Usefulness of Seeing Projects as Action Learning Cycles

What is the potential impact of this research?	To improve the capacity of project management team members to become reflective practitioners and to improve knowledge transfer within and between projects and programs.
How can it be useful to the project management profession?	Improved knowledge transfer from one team to another, from project to project, and from project to program, could significantly reduce wasted effort and resources. Seeing projects as action learning cycles also permits great competence and skill upgrades for all concerned.

growth and, in fact, inhibits it or is toxic in some way. In the traditional project management context, knowledge may be seen as a largely irrelevant project output even if it may be a "nice to have" outcome. Often, people see no need to reflect or to exchange perspectives on issues beyond immediate problem-solving when necessary, so knowledge becomes undervalued and is given a low priority as a useful, tradeable, and convertible asset. Szulanski also identified poor absorptive capacity as another barrier to effective knowledge transfer. Cohen and Levinthal (1990) define absorptive capacity as the ability of a firm to recognize the value of new external information, assimilate it, and use it for commercial ends. It is a measure of an ability to absorb ideas, information, and knowledge and applies to both external and internal sources of information and knowledge.

6.2.1.5 Subsection Summary

We selected four implications of the work to discuss and to answer the question posed at the start of this chapter from the perspective of being valuable to the practitioner. While we discussed four implications, there are many more that we could elaborate on; space constraints have forced us to select those we felt most relevant to the theme of this book.

6.2.2 Impact and Implications for Project Management Scholarship

Again, we have selected the four most relevant impacts and implications for project management scholarship, as illustrated below:

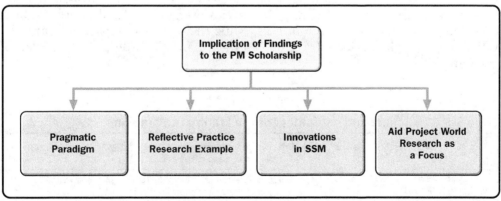

Figure 6-2   High Level Summary of Research Implications to Project Management Scholarship

6.2.2.1   The Pragmatic Paradigm

At the start of this book, we emphasized that both Paul and Derek arrive in project management scholarship from a background of strong and lengthy industry practice, and both also from a very traditional part of the project management world—the construction and engineering sectors. This gave us the propensity to hold a positivist stance on many issues and we tended to see projects through a plan-and-control and more technical perspective. That would be our "default" position because most of our experience has been in these "earth"-type projects. However, both of us have shifted positions quite radically over the past decade and become increasingly engaged in the "soft" or people side of project management, so we also gravitate toward an interpretist perspective of trying to make sense of what happens in project work.

While this may appear somewhat inconsistent, and even schizophrenic, we don't see that holding both those views simultaneously is necessarily a problem. This is really about managing complementarities, and there has been some substantial academic work that supports the value of this way of seeing the world (Milgrom & Roberts, 1995; Whittington, Pettigrew, Peck, Fenton, & Conyon, 1999; Massini & Pettigrew, 2003; Pettigrew & Whittington, 2003; Whittington & Pettigrew, 2003; Cozzarin & Percival, 2006).

Chapter 3 provides our justification, so we do not need to repeat it here. We now address the questions posed at the start of this chapter, as illustrated in Table 6-5.

When we reviewed the literature that we presented in Section 3.3.3 in particular, we found that pragmatism is a well-established paradigm. Being pragmatic means that you tend to believe more in what seems to work when it is justified by valid evidence. We suggested above in Section 6.2.1.3 that the necessary evidence for this justification is that its criteria should facilitate *knowledge and understanding/sense-making,* be *practical and workable,* demonstrate *community internal/external validity,* and produce an *objective impact* on the research being undertaken.

We found the pragmatism concept to be very useful, and it formed Paul's idea to measure each action learning cycle (refer to Table 4-3, for example). These four criteria are derived from pragmatic action research evaluation theory. Workability and sense-making are primarily pragmatic tests. However, internal and external validation stems from action research origins, while the objective impact is, primarily, validation through "evaluation" (Hope & Waterman, 2003; Brook, 2004; Eden & Huxham, 2006; York, 2009).

Table 6-5   Impact and Usefulness of the Pragmatic Paradigm

What is the potential impact of this research?	To improve interest in, and quality of, project management research through accepting a pragmatic paradigm as valid.
How can it be useful to the project management profession?	It could motivate more highly experienced scholars with highly valuable lived experience of project management to make their contributions using a pragmatic approach and to cite Paul's work and the authorities that he cites to justify this stance.

Table 6-6   Impact and Usefulness of Reflective Research

What is the potential impact of this research?	To improve understanding of the fine-grained complexities experienced by project managers – their lived experience.
How can it be useful to the project management profession?	It could unearth many instances of tacit knowledge and expose the raw, lived experience in such a way that emotions, feelings, and power issues are far more clearly portrayed than in many other research approaches.

6.2.2.2   Reflective Practice as a Research Approach Exemplar

Calls for reflective practice as an approach to research are not new (Schön, 1983; Raelin, 2007). However, there still seems to be a residual suspicion among many academics that practitioners cannot be trusted to base findings on intuition. The medical profession, which has had several hundred years of theory development from, and out of, practice, has built its reputation through studies of reflection on cases in a way which exposes assumptions that may have turned out to herald misplaced confidence in a theory. For some unexplained reason, project management and many management discipline domains are expected to conform to scientific paradigms of "truth" and "rigor in research," even though management is dealing with social systems rather than mechanical or molecular interactions.

Reflection and sense-making have been championed and advanced by such proponents as Raelin (2001; 2007) and Weick (2001b; Weick et al., 2005), so they have strong pedigrees. This work supports that tradition and adds to numerous studies of the lived experience of project managers, such as that found throughout the chapters of Hodgson and Cicmil's book (2006). Table 6-6 illustrates our answers to this chapter's questions.

This work also provides a high level of reflective practitioner research, with reflections from Paul, which span 40 years, from his CoP member reflective practice input, as well as from the very valuable SSM studies.

6.2.2.3   Innovations in SSM

Some of the more exciting outcomes from this research were the innovations that Paul developed while pragmatically facing challenges in conducting interviews with very busy, absorbed professional project team members and operating in distressing conditions. The "normal" SSM practice is to interview participants and, over time, develop rich pictures through an iterative process.

In the action learning Cycle 2, Paul needed to actually travel to some wild and dangerous parts of Indonesia to interview the participants. This was hazardous and, in fact, Paul ended up contracting a tropical virus as a consequence during one visit, so he had to find ways of doing fieldwork that maximized feedback and co-development of the rich pictures, while still retaining standards of rigor and the ethical observance of the participants' political and work relationship conditions.

He managed to devise a way to co-develop, with his participants, a means of representing the classical cartoon-like vignettes, while overlaying these with themes and action-related color coding (see the description of this in the action learning Cycle 2, Section 4.4, and the description of contribution in Section 5.2.5). These were significant innovations, in that they provided ideas as to how rich pictures can be drawn (and used for the co-generation and review they entail) in a way that intensifies meaning

Table 6-7   Impact and Usefulness of Innovations in SSM

What is the potential impact of this research?	To improve the efficiency and effectiveness of developing rich pictures in SSM studies.
How can it be useful to the project management profession?	The approach to investigating messy situations using SSM becomes a useful general tool that can be used not only by researchers but also by practitioners in problem-solving. The innovations of color-coding themes and important processes add to the clarity of the rich pictures and make developing root definitions more straightforward.

and imparts themes and issues with distinct clarity. Paul also used technology effectively by utilizing emails to pass evolving versions of the rich picture over an extended period, until the participant was happy to sign off on the veracity of each picture.

Paul's extensive and rigorous experience as a project manager forced him to take this approach. This was because his entire life's experience of project management had been about working with stakeholders. For decades he has been used to gaining other people's perception of "truth"—be it the expected time to undertake some task, the method to perform some complicated operation or to gain acceptance for a plan of action, or the sensitive negotiation over issues. Again, he took a pragmatic approach, and his criteria for what worked and what did not were precisely those five criteria presented earlier, in Section 6.2.2.1. Table 6-7 illustrates the impact and usefulness of these innovations.

This contribution to SSM innovation had dual utility in being useful for general research as a way of improving how to develop rich pictures, while at the same time being an exemplar of how SSM can be used in decision making, thus building on other useful examples that we highlighted in Section 3.3.2 (see examples from Checkland & Winter, 2006; Winter, 2009).

6.2.2.4   Aid Project World Research as a Focus

This research cited only a few examples of project management research being undertaken within the aid relief project world, compared to the plethora of research case studies on construction or IT projects, and even change management or business process change, which may be found. What this research brings to the traditional project management community is reinforcement that worthy research should be taken, that aid world tools such as LogFrame and M&E are worthy of further study from a project management perspective, and that a project management perspective on aid projects could be very rewarding. Table 6-8 illustrates the impact and usefulness of research aid relief projects.

Table 6-8   Impact and Usefulness of Undertaking Aid Relief Project Research

What is the potential impact of this research?	To demonstrate how aid projects can be studied from a project management perspective. To show how studies can be used to validate tools and techniques either from the aid relief project world or from the traditional project management world.
How can it be useful to the project management profession?	The methodology of action learning Cycle 2, as well as of action learning Cycle 3, is useful as a validation approach.

We hope that this outcome of the research will prompt testing of LogFrame and M&E in a variety of other project management contexts, and that our study will prompt other scholars to investigate the lived experience of project managers in this highly challenging environment.

6.2.2.5 Subsection Summary

We selected four implications of the work to discuss and answer the questions posed at the start of this chapter from the perspective of their value to research. There are many more implications that we could elaborate on, but, once again, space constraints have forced us to select those we felt most relevant to the theme of this book.

6.3 Concluding Comments

In Chapter 1, we answered the questions of why we do projects and with what purpose. This was extensively discussed in Section 1.2.

6.3.1. Practice and Scholarship Contributions Made

We then set out a series of contribution objectives that we aimed to achieve through presenting our research in this book. These are summarized in Table 6-9, with details of where each was addressed.

We also draw the reader's attention to Table 4-1 in Section 4.2, in which we detailed Paul's thesis objective of understanding the antecedents of project management best practice through lessons learned from the aid relief project world, with three identified outcomes and specific actions for each outcome. These actions informed the research-oriented action research that provides the empirical evidence to support the research conclusions and assessment of impact.

Table 6-9   Contributions Made in This Book Through the Research Reported on

Contribution	Where this is made in the book
1. Explaining how the project management mindset is changing to enable us to better see value and benefit as being derived from individual projects, to (most usually) enhance the effectiveness of programs designed to deliver business or social outcomes.	Sections 2.3, 2.4, 2.5, and Table 5-4 in Section 5.2.7.
2. Offering a deeper understanding of the validity of seeing project objectives and outputs in a broader way than has been traditionally privileged and dominant in the project management literature, through our exposure to the vast aid relief and aid project literature.	Section 2.6 and throughout Chapter 4.
3. Introducing pragmatic research methodological approaches to readers who may not have considered their usefulness before.	This was pursued with vigor in Chapter 3, particularly in Section 3.3.3, as well as in Chapter 5, and in Section 6.2.1.1 in Chapter 6.
4. Exploring the lived experience of project managers in extraordinarily challenging circumstances; indicating how they cope and what other project management professionals in more traditional contexts can learn from them.	Chapter 4 through each of the action learning cycles, but particularly in Cycle 2 through the rich pictures.
5. Explaining the nature and impact of the antecedents of project management best practice.	Chapter 5 and Section 6.2 in Chapter 6.

6.3.2 Future Directions

Where to from here? There is still much to do. The value articulated in this book strongly suggests that more empirical work can, and should, be undertaken by "pracademics" using their "lived experience" to guide explorations of project management practice in a variety of settings. This study primarily drew upon aid relief projects to inform differences in project management practices between construction/engineering projects and aid relief projects. The comparison unearthed insights into the environmental differences between these two types of projects and indicated that the Cynefyn Framework (Snowden & Boone, 2007) discussed in Section 2.7.1 was a useful way to see how ordered, unordered, and disordered contexts shape leadership approaches.

For example, the literature on project management work in managing networks of organizations (Artto & Kujala, 2008) provides fertile ground for an action learning study such as this. More work on business transformations that adds to a recent study by another "pracademic" from the Logistics and Transport project arena (Arroyo, 2009; Arroyo & Walker, 2009) could be undertaken using the SSM approach explained in detail in this book. A recent special edition of the *Journal of Media Business Studies* edited (and with an interesting paper written) by Lundin (2009) provided a series of interesting papers based on the lived experience of television producers and others working in project management type roles in temporary organizations established to produce television and films. The Internet and visual digital media world now have a host of project management teams producing games, simulation software, and many other interesting media project outputs.

Much of government and delivery of social services is now being seen as project work with erstwhile operation managers being rebirthed as project managers who are coping with managing temporary organizations in ways that are alien to many of them. We need to learn more about their "lived experience" of project management and what lessons they can bring to the more traditional project management world in the same way that this study allowed us to (re)discover long-established tools and techniques such as LogFrame and M&E that, while known in the project management literature, nevertheless lie at its fringe at present.

Finally, the pragmatic approach from a research methods perspective is still viewed with suspicion in many quarters as not being "real science" or even valid "social science," so more empirical work that is demonstrably rigorous needs to be done to gain greater acceptance of the pragmatic paradigm in research that deals with practical matters affecting our quality of life, such as this study has done.

6.4 Chapter Summary

This chapter had the objectives of concluding the book in a neat fashion, while leaving readers with the sense that this does not represent the final step in a journey, but rather the necessary preparatory steps to be taken to begin one.

The chapter highlighted four major implications that the research has for project management practice and scholarship. These were not exhaustive, but rather indicative, and other implications could also be drawn. We tried to clearly establish the impact made by this research and how it may be useful to project management.

We hope that other researchers will continue this type of work and that it provides a useful exemplar. Our short section on future directions should stimulate that interest.

In wrapping up this book, we again acknowledge the contributions made by Paul's CoP. They have been patient and intensely valuable as a sounding board and as an expert group that helped to dynamically reframe insights and explore the impact and validity of the research findings discussed and presented here.

If there is one concluding point that we wish to make for other "pracademics," it is that the strength in research rigor of engaging a voluntary CoP is beyond measure. This in itself has been somewhat of an experiment. Derek, as an experienced doctoral thesis supervisor, had never seen this approach used in such a way, and to him it appeared at times over the three-year journey that he and Paul were indeed lucky to have had a Delphi-like group participating throughout. We hope, therefore, that those CoP members who read this book will realize that their contributions were of much value.

References

Aaltonen, K., Jaakko, K., & Tuomas, O. (2008). Stakeholder salience in global projects. *International Journal of Project Management, 26*(5), 509–516.

Aaltonen, K., & Sivonen, R. (2009). Response strategies to stakeholder pressures in global projects. *International Journal of Project Management, 27*(2), 131–141.

Andersen, E. S. (1996). Warning: Activity planning is hazardous to your project's health! *International Journal of Project Management, 14*(2), 89–94.

Andersen, E. S. (2006). Toward a project management theory for renewal projects. *Project Management Journal, 37*(4), 15–30.

Andersen, E. S. (2008). *Rethinking project management:An organisational perspective.* Harlow, UK: Pearson Education Limited.

Andersen, E. S., Grude, K. V., & Haug, T. (1995). *Goal directed project management.* London: Kogan Page.

Anderson, C., & McMillan, E. (2003). Of ants and men: Self-organized teams in human and insect organizations. *Emergence, 5*(2), 29–41.

Anderson, J. C., Narus, J. A., & van Rossum, W. (2006). Customer value propositions in business markets. *Harvard Business Review, 84*(3), 90–99.

Archer, N. P., & Ghasemzadeh, F. (1999). An integrated framework for project portfolio selection. *International Journal of Project Management, 17*(4), 207–216.

Argyris, C., & Schön, D. A. (1974). *Theory in practice: Increasing professional effectiveness* (1st ed.). San Francisco: Jossey-Bass.

Argyris, C., & Schön, D. A. (1996). *Organizational learning II: Theory, method, and practice.* Reading, MA: Addison-Wesley.

Arroyo, A. C. (2009). *The role of the Atlantic Corridor Project as a form of strategic community of practice in facilitating business transformations in Latin America.* Unpublished doctoral dissertation, RMIT University—Melbourne.

Arroyo, A. C., & Walker, D. H. T. (2009, May). *A Latin American strategic organisational transformation project management experience: The motivation to transform business.* Paper presented at the conference of the European Academy of Management (EURAM): Renaissance and Renewal in Management Studies, Liverpool.

Artto, K., & Kujala, J. (2008). Project business as a research field. *International Journal of Managing Projects in Business, 1*(4), 469–497.

Artto, K., Martinsuo, M., Dietrich, P., & Kujala, J. (2008). Project strategy: Strategy types and their contents in innovation projects. *International Journal of Managing Projects in Business, 1*(1), 49–70.

Artto, K., Martinsuo, M., Gemünden, H. G., & Murtoaro, J. (2009). Foundations of program management: A bibliometric view. *International Journal of Project Management, 27*(1), 1–18.

Atkinson, R. (1999). Project management: Cost, time, and quality, two best guesses and a phenomenon; it's time to accept other success criteria. *International Journal of Project Management, 17*(6), 337–342.

Attwater, R. (1999). Pragmatism, philosophy, and soft systems in an Upland Thai catchment. *System Research and Behavioral Science, 16*(4), 299–209.

Aubry, M., Hobbs, B., & Thuillier, D. (2008). Organisational project management: An historical approach to the study of PMOs. *International Journal of Project Management, 26*(1), 38–43.

AusAID (2005). *AusGuide: A guide to program management; AusGuideline 3.3: The logical framework approach* [Brochure]. Canberra, Commonwealth of Australia: Author.

AusAID (2007). *Performance assessment and evaluation policy.* Retrieved November 10, 2010, from http://www.ausaid.gov.au/ode/pdf/performance_policy.pdf

Australian Council for International Development. (2009). *ACFID code of conduct: For non government development organizations.* Deakin ACT, Australia: Author.

Avolio, B. (1996). What's all the karping about down under? In W. Parry K. W. (Ed.), *Leadership research and practice* (pp. 3–15). South Melbourne: Pitman Publishing.

Avolio, B. J., & Bass, B. M. (1995). Individual consideration viewed at multiple levels of analysis: A multi-level framework for examining the diffusion of transformational leadership. *The Leadership Quarterly, 6*(2), 199–218.

Avolio, B. J., & Gardner, W. L. (2005). Authentic leadership development: Getting to the root of positive forms of leadership. *The Leadership Quarterly, 16*(3), 315–338.

Avolio, B. J., Gardner, W. L., Walumbwa, F. L., & May, D. R. (2004). Unlocking the mask: A look at the process by which authentic leaders impact follower attitudes and behaviors. *Leadership Quarterly, 15*, 801–823.

Avolio, B. J., & Locke, E. E. (2002). Contrasting different philosophies of leader motivation: Altruism versus egoism. *The Leadership Quarterly, 13*(2), 169–191.

Avolio, B. J., & Luthans, F. (2006). *The high impact leader: Moments matter in accelerating authentic leadership development.* New York: McGraw Hill.

Baccarini, D. (1996). The concept of project complexity: A review. *International Journal of Project Management, 14*(4), 201–204.

Baccarini, D. (1999). The logical framework method for defining project success. *Project Management Journal, 30*(4), 25–32.

Bachy, G., & Hameri, A. P. (1997). What has to be implemented at the early stages of a large-scale project. *International Journal of Project Management, 15*(4), 211–218.

Bass, B. M. (1985). Leadership: Good, better, best. *Organizational Dynamics, 13*(3), 26–40.

Baum, W. C. (1978). The World Bank project cycle. *Finance & Development, 15*(4), 10–17.

Bentley, C. (1997). *PRINCE 2: A practical handbook.* Oxford, UK: Butterworth-Heinemann.

Binnendijk, A. (2000). *Results based management in the development co-operation agencies: A review of experience, background report.* (158) Paris, France: Development Assistance Committee (DAC) Working Party on Aid Evaluation OECD Development Cooperation Directorate.

Blamey, A., & Mackenzie, M. (2007). Theories of change and realistic evaluation: Peas in a pod or apples and oranges? *Evaluation, 13,* 439–455.

Bluedorn, A. C., & Waller, M. J. (2006). The stewardship of the temporal commons. *Research in Organizational Behavior, 27,* 355–396.

Bonabeau, E., & Meyer, C. (2001). Swarm intelligence: A whole new way to think about business. *Harvard Business Review, 79*(5), 106–114.

Bourne, L. (2005). *Project relationship management and the stakeholder circle.* Unpublished doctoral dissertation, RMIT University—Melbourne.

Bourne, L. (2008). Advancing theory and practice for successful implementation of stakeholder management in organisations. *International Journal of Managing Projects in Business. 1*(4), 587–601.

Bourne, L., & Walker, D. H. T. (2005). Visualising and mapping stakeholder influence. *Management Decision, 43*(5), 649–660.

Bourne, L., & Walker, D. H. T. (2006). Using a visualising tool to study stakeholder influence: Two Australian examples. *Journal of Project Management, 37*(1), 5–21.

Bourne, L. M. (2009). *Stakeholder relationship management.* Farnham, Surrey, UK: Gower.

Bradley, G. (2006). *Benefit realisation management.* Aldershot, UK: Gower.

Brady, T., & Davies, A. (2004). Building project capabilities: From exploratory to exploitative learning. *Organization Studies, 25*(9), 1601–1621.

Brook, P. (2004). *Constituents and their expectation: Towards a critical-pragmatic theory of information systems project management.* Unpublished doctoral dissertation, University of Western Sydney—Sydney, Australia.

Carr, W. (2006). Philosophy, methodology and action research. *Journal of Philosophy of Education, 40*(4), 421–435.

Carr, W., & Kemmis, S. (1986). *Becoming critical: education, knowledge and action research, Rev. ed.,* Waurn Ponds, Vic., Australia, Deakin University : distributed by Deakin University Press.

Carroll, A. B., & Buchholtz, A. K. (2000). *Business and society: Ethics and stakeholder management.* Cincinnati, OH: South-Western College Publishing.

Carroll, J. B., & McKenna, J. (2001). Theory to practice: Using the logic model to organize and report research results in a collaborative project. *Journal of Family and Consumer Sciences, 93*(4), 63–65.

Cartwright, C., & Walker, D. H. T. (2008). Case study: Developing a centre of excellence (CoE). In D. H. T. Walker & S. Rowlinson (Eds.), *Procurement systems: A cross industry project management perspective* (pp. 358–377). Abingdon, Oxon: Taylor & Francis.

Checkland, P. (1999). *Systems thinking, systems practice.* Chichester, UK: John Wiley & Sons Ltd.

Checkland, P. (2000). Soft systems methodology: A thirty-year retrospective. *Systems Research and Behavioral Science, 17,* S11-S58.

Checkland, P., & Winter, M. (2006). Process and content: Two ways of using SSM. *The Journal of the Operational Research Society, 57*(12), 1435–1441.

Christenson, D. (2007). *Using vision as a critical success element in project management.* Unpublished doctoral dissertation, RMIT University—Melbourne.

Christenson, D., & Walker, D. H. T. (2003, June). *Project stewardship: The convergence of project leadership and management.* Paper presented at the 17th World Congress on Project Management, Moscow, Russia. On CD-ROM.

Christenson, D., & Walker, D. H. T. (2004). Understanding the role of "vision" in project success. *Project Management Journal, 35*(3), 39–52.

Cicmil, S. (2003). *From instrumental rationality to practical wisdom.* Leicester: Salmon de Montfort.

Cicmil, S. (2006). Understanding project management practice through interpretative and critical research perspectives. *Project Management Journal, 37*(2), 27–37.

Clarke, N., & Howell, R. (2009). *Emotional intelligence and projects.* Newtown Square, PA: Project Management Institute.

Cohen, W. M., & Levinthal, D. (1990). Absorptive capacity: A new perspective on learning and innovation. *Administrative Science Quarterly, 35*(1), 128–152.

Collins, J. (2001). Level 5 leadership: The triumph of humility and fierce resolve. *Harvard Business Review, 79*(1), 66–76.

Cooke-Davies, T. (2002). The "real" success factors on projects. *International Journal of Project Management, 20*(3), 185–190.

Cooper, R. G. (2005). *Product leadership: Pathways to profitable innovation.* New York: Basic Books.

Cooper, R. G., Edgett, S. J., & Kleinschmidt, E. J. (1997). Portfolio management in new product development: Lessons from the leaders. *Research Technology Management, 40*(5), 16–28.

Cozzarin, B. P., & Percival, J. C. (2006). Complementarities between organisational strategies and innovation. *Economics of Innovation and New Technology, 15*(3), 195–217.

Crawford, L., & Cooke-Davies, T. J. (2006, August). *Project governance: The role and capabilities of the executive sponsor.* Paper presented at Achieving Excellence, Moscow, Russia. On CD-ROM.

Crawford, L., Morris, P., Thomas, J., & Winter, M. (2006). Practitioner development: From trained technicians to reflective practitioners. *International Journal of Project Management, 24*(8), 722–733.

Crawford, P. (2004b). *Aiding Aid: A monitoring & evaluation framework to enhance international aid effectiveness.* Unpublished doctoral dissertation, University of Technology—Sydney, Australia.

Crawford, P., & Bryce, P. (2003). Project monitoring and evaluation: A method for enhancing the efficiency and effectiveness of aid project implementation. *International Journal of Project Management, 21*(5), 363–373.

Crist, J. D., Parsons, M. L., Warner-Robbins, C., & Mullins, M. V. (2009). Pragmatic action research with 2 vulnerable populations: Mexican American elders and formerly incarcerated women. *Fam Community Health, 32*(4), 320–329.

Dainty, A. R. J., Bryman, A., Price, A. D. F., Greasley, K., Soetanto, R., & King, N. (2005). Project affinity: The role of emotional attachment in construction projects. *Construction Management & Economics, 23*(3), 241–244.

Dainty, A. R. J., Cheng, M. I., & Moore, D. R. (2004). A competency-based performance model for construction project managers. *Construction Management & Economics, 22*(8), 877–888.

Davis, J. H., Schoorman, D. F., & Donaldson, L. (1997). Towards a stewardship theory of management. *Academy of Management Review, 22*(1), 20–48.

de Wit, A. (1988). Measurement of project success. *International Journal of Project Management, 6*(3), 164–170.

Delisle, C. L., & Thomas, J. L. (2002). Success: Getting traction in a turbulent business climate. In D. P., Sleven, D. I. Cleland, & J. K. Pinto (Eds.) *The frontiers of project management* (Research Conference Proceedings). Newtown Square, PA: Project Management Institute.

Dewey, J. (1929). *The quest for certainty: The study of the relation of knowledge and action.* London: George Allen & Unwin Ltd.

Diallo, A., & Thuillier, D. (2004). The success dimensions of international development projects: The perceptions of African project coordinators. *International Journal of Project Management, 22*(1), 19–31.

Diallo, A., & Thuillier, D. (2005). The success of international development projects, trust, and communication: An African perspective. *International Journal of Project Management, 23*(3), 237–252.

Dick, B. (2002a). AR as meta-research. *International Sociological Association Conference.* Brisbane: 1–12.

Dick, B. (2002b). Postgraduate programs using action research. *The Learning Organization, 9*(4), 159–170.

Dick, B. (2009). Action research literature 2006–2008: Themes and trends. *Action Research, 7*(4), 423–441.

Dick, B., Stringer, E., & Huxham, C. (2009). Theory in action research. *Action Research, 7*(5), 5–12.

Donaldson, T., & Preston, L. E. (1995). The stakeholder theory of the corporation: Concepts, evidence, and implications. *Academy of Management Review, 20*(1), 65–91.

Doty, A. (2008). An examination of the value of the Victorian government's investment logic map as a tool for front-end evaluation of investment proposals. *Evaluation Journal of Australasia, 8*(1), 26–139.

Dreyfus, H. L., & Dreyfus, S. E. (2005). Expertise in real world contexts. *Organization Studies (01708406), 26*(5), 779–792.

Earle, L. (2003, March-April). *Lost in the matrix: The LogFrame and the local picture.* Paper presented at INTRAC's 5th Evaluation Conference: Measurement, management and accountability?, The Netherlands. INTERAC: 17pp.

Eden, C., & Huxham, C. (2006). Researching organizations using action research. In S. Clegg, C. Hardy, W. Nord & T. Lawrence (Eds.), *Handbook of organisation studies* (pp. 526–542). Beverly Hills, CA: Sage.

Eikeland, O. (2007). From epistemology to gnoseology: Understanding the knowledge claims of action research. *Management Research News, 30*(5), 344–358.

Englund, R. L., & Bucero, A. (2006). *Project sponsorship: Achieving management commitment for project success.* San Francisco: Jossey-Bass.

Evaristo, R., & van Fenema, P. C. (1999). A typology of project management: Emergence and evolution of new forms. *International Journal of Project Management, 17*(5), 275–281.

Finch, P. (2003). Applying the Slevin-Pinto Project Implementation Profile to an information systems project. *Project Management Journal, 34*(3), 32.

Fishman, D. B., & Neigher, W. D. (2003). Publishing systematic, pragmatic case studies in program evaluation: Rationale and introduction to the special issue. *Evaluation and Program Planning, 26*, 421–428.

Flyvbjerg, B., Holm, M. S., & Buhl, S. (2002). Underestimating costs in public works projects: Error or lie? *Journal of the American Planning Association, 68*(3), 279.

Flyvbjerg, B., Rothengatter, W., & Bruzelius, N. (2003). *Megaprojects and risk: An anatomy of ambition.* New York: Cambridge University Press.

Gareis, R. (1989). "Management by projects:" The management approach for the future. *International Journal of Project Management, 7*(4), 243–249.

George, B., Sims, P., McLean, A. N., & Mayer, D. (2007). Discovering your authentic leadership. *Harvard Business Review, 85*(2), 129–138.

Gharajedaghi, J. (2006). Systems thinking: Managing chaos and complexity: A platform for designing business architecture (2nd ed.). New York, NY: Elsevier.

Gharajedaghi, J. (2007). System thinking: A case for second order learning. *The Learning Organization, 14*(6), 473–479.

Gharajedaghi. J., & Ackoff, R. (1984). Mechanisms, organisms and social systems. *Strategic Management Journal, 5,* 289–300.

Glaser, B. G., & Strauss, A. L. (1967). *The discovery of grounded theory: Strategies for Qualitative Research.* New York: Aldine Publishing Company.

Goleman, D. (1995). *Emotional intelligence.* New York: Bantam Books.

Goleman, D. (1999). *Working with emotional intelligence.* London: Bloomsbury.

Goleman, D. (2000). Leadership that gets results. *Harvard Business Review, 78*(2), 78–90.

Goleman, D., Boyatzis, R. E., & McKee, A. (2002). *The new leaders: Transforming the art of leadership into the science of results.* London: Little Brown.

Green, S. D. (1999). A participative research strategy for propagating soft methodologies in value management practice. *Construction Management and Economics, 17*(3), 329–340.

Green, S. D., & Simister, S. J. (1999). Modeling client business processes as an aid to strategic briefing. *Construction Management and Economics, 17*(1), 63–76.

Greenfield, S. (2001). *Brain Story* [Video]. Sydney, Australia: Australian Broadcasting Corporation.

Helm, J., & Remington, K. (2005). Effective project sponsorship: An evaluation of the role of the executive sponsor in complex infrastructure projects by senior project managers. *Project Management Journal, 36*(3), 51–61.

Hersey, P., Blanchard, K., & Johnson, D. E. (1996). *Management of organizational behaviour.* London: Prentice Hall International.

Hobbs, B., & Aubry, M. (2007). A multi-phase research program investigating project management offices (PMOs): The results of phase 1. *Project Management Journal, 38*(1), 74–86.

Hobbs, B., & Aubry, M. (2008). An empirically grounded search for a typology of project management offices. *Project Management Journal, 39*(S1), S69-S82.

Hodgson, D., & Cicmil, S. (2006). *Making projects critical.* Basingstoke, UK: Palgrave MacMillan.

Hofstede, G. (1991). *Culture and organizations: Software of the mind.* New York: McGraw-Hill.

Hope, K. W., & Waterman, H. A. (2003). Praiseworthy pragmatism? Validity and action research. *Journal of Advanced Nursing, 44*(2), 120–127.

House, R., Javidan, M., Hanges, P., & Dorfman, P. (2002). Understanding cultures and implicit leadership theories across the globe: An introduction to project GLOBE. *Journal of World Business, 37*(1), 3–10.

Hughes, I., Ndonko, F., Ouedraogo, B., Ngum, J., & Popp, D. (2004). International education for action research: The Bamenda model. *Action Research e-Reports. 020,* 15pp

Hyväri, I. (2006). Success of projects in different organizational conditions. *Project Management Journal, 37*(4), 31–41.

Ika, L. A., Diallo, A., & Thuillier, D. (2009). Project management in the international development industry: The project coordinator's perspective. *International Journal of Managing Projects in Business, 3*(1), 61–93.

IMF. (2007). *Manual on fiscal transparency glossary of statistical terms.* Retrieved June 1, 2010, from http://stats.oecd.org/glossary/detail.asp?ID57311

Jaafari, A. (2003). Project management in the age of complexity and change. *Project Management Journal, 34*(4), 47–57.

Jackson, B. (1997). *Designing projects and project evaluations using the logical framework approach.* Retrieved November 10, 2010, from the International Union for the Conservation of Nature and Natural Resources (IUCN) Web site: http://cmsdata.iucn.org/downloads/logframepaper3.pdf

Johansson, A. W., & Lindhult, E. (2008). Emancipation or workability? Critical versus pragmatic scientific orientation in action research. *Action Research, 6*(1), 95–115.

Jones, C., Hesterly, W. S., & Borgatti, S. P. (1997). A general theory of network governance: Exchange conditions and social mechanisms. *Academy of Management Review, 22*(4), 911–145.

Jones, T. M., & Wicks, A. C. (1999). Convergent stakeholder theory. *Academy of Management Review, 24*(2), 206–221.

Keegan, A. E., & Den Hartog, D. N. (2004). Transformational leadership in a project-based environment: A comparative study of the leadership styles of project managers and line managers. *International Journal of Project Management, 22*(8), 609–617.

Kemmis, S., & McTaggart, R. (1988). *The action research planner.* Victoria, Australia: Deakin University Press.

Khang, D. B., & Moe, T. L. (2008). Success criteria and factors for international development projects: A life-cycle-based framework. *Project Management Journal, 39*(1), 72–84.

Klakegg, O. J. (2010). Governance of major public investment projects in pursuit of relevance and sustainability. Unpublished doctoral dissertation, Norwegian University of Science and Technology—Trondheim.

Klakegg, O. J., Williams, T., Walker, D. H. T., Andersen, B., & Magnussen, O. M. (2011). *Early warning signs in complex projects.* Newtown Square, PA: Project Management Institute.

Kolb, D. A. (1984). *Experiential learning: Experience as the source of learning and development.* Englewood Cliffs, NJ: Prentice-Hall.

Koskinen, K. U. (2009). Project-based company's vital condition: Structural coupling, an autopoietic view. *Knowledge and Process Management, 16*(1), 13–22.

Koskinen, K. U. (2010). *Autopoitic knowledge systems in project-based companies.* London: Palgrave Macmillan.

Koskinen, K. U., & Aramo-Immonen, H. (2008). Remembering with the help of personal notes in a project work context. *International Journal of Managing Projects in Business, 1*(2), 193–205.

Koskinen, K. U., & Mäkinen, S. (2009). Role of boundary objects in negotiations of project contracts. *International Journal of Project Management, 27*(1), 31–38.

Koskinen, K. U., & Pihlanto, P. (2006). Competence transfer from old timers to newcomers analysed with the help of the holistic concept of man. *Knowledge and Process Management, 13*(1), 3–12.

Koskinen, K. U., Pihlanto, P., & Vanharanta, H. (2003). Tacit knowledge acquisition and sharing in a project work context. *International Journal of Project Management, 21*(4), 281–290.

KPMG. (2003). *Programme management survey: Why keep punishing your bottom line?* (General Report No. 20). Singapore: KPMG International Asia-Pacific.

Kusek, J. Z., & Rist, R. C. (2004). *Ten steps to a results-based monitoring and evaluation system: A handbook for development practitioners.* Washington D.C.: Office of the Publisher, World Bank.

Kvale, S. (1995). The social construction of validity. *Qualitative Inquiry, 1*(1), 19–40.

Larsen, K., & Cottrell, A. (2006, July). *Action research: The underlying approach of the Understanding Communities Project (C1) within the Bushfire Cooperative Research Center* (Briefing Paper). Townsville, Queensland: James Cook University, Bushfire CRC.

Lau, F. (1999). Toward a framework for action research in information systems studies. *Information Technology & People, 12*(2), 148–175.

Lauriol, J. (2006). Proposals for designing and controlling a doctoral research project in management sciences. *The Electronic Journal of Business Research Methods, 4*(1), 31–38.

Lave, J., & Wenger, E. C. (1991). *Situated learning: Legitimate peripheral participation.* Cambridge: Cambridge University Press.

Levin, G., & Green, A. R. (2008). *Implementing program management templates and forms aligned with the standard for program management.* Boca Raton, FL: CRC Press.

Lloyd-Walker, B. M., & Walker, D. H. T. (2010, May). *Authentic leadership for 21st century project delivery.* Paper presented at the European Academy of Management EURAM: Back to the Future, Rome.

Locke, K. D. (2001). *Grounded theory in management research.* London and Thousand Oaks, CA: Sage Publications.

Long, N. D., Ogunlana, S., Quang, T., & Lam, K. C. (2004). Large construction projects in developing countries: A case study from Vietnam. *International Journal of Project Management, 22*(7), 553–561.

Lundin, R. (2009). Managing projects in the TV production industry: The case of Sweden. *Journal of Media Business Studies, 6*(4), 103–121.

Luthans, F., & Youssef, C. M. (2004). Human, social, and now positive psychological capital management: Investing in people for competitive advantage. *Organizational Dynamics, 33*(2), 143–160.

Maccoby, M. (2000). Narcissistic leaders. *Harvard Business Review, 78*(1), 68–77.

Maqsood, T. (2006). The role of knowledge management in supporting innovation and learning in construction. Unpublished doctoral dissertation, RMIT University—Melbourne.

Maqsood, T., Finegan, A., & Walker, D. H. T. (2003, December). *A soft approach to solving hard problems in construction project management.* Paper presented at the second International Conference on Construction in the 21st Century, Hong Kong. (CDROM ISBN: 988-07370-1-9): 312–317.

Massini, S., & Pettigrew, A. (2003). Complementarities in organizational innovation and performance: Evidence from the INNFORM survey. In A. M. Pettigrew, R. Whittington, L. Melin, C. Sánchez-Runde, F. A. J. van den Bosch, W. Ruigrok, & T. Numagami (Eds.) *Innovative forms of organizing* (pp. 133–172). Thousand Oaks, CA: Sage.

Maula, M. (2000). The senses and memory of a firm: Implications of autopoiesis theory for knowledge management. *Journal of Knowledge Management, 4*(2), 157–161.

McNiff, J., & Whitehead, J. (2000). *Action research in organisations.* London: Routledge.

Melles, G. (2008). An enlarged pragmatist inquiry paradigm for methodological pluralism in academic design research. *Artifact, 2*(1), 3–11.

Melles, G. (2009). Teaching and evaluation of critical appraisal skills to post-graduate ESL engineering students. *Innovations in Education and Teaching International, 46*(2), 161–170.

Melrose, M. J. (2001). Maximising the rigor of action research: Why would you want to? How could you? *Field Methods, 13*(2), 160–180.

Meyer, J. P., & Allen, N. J. (1991). A three-component conceptualization of organizational commitment. *Human Resource Management Review, 1*(1), 61–89.

Milgrom, P. R., & Roberts, J. (1995). Complementarities and fit strategy, structure, and organizational change in manufacturing. *Journal of Accounting and Economics, 19*(2/3), 179–208.

Miller, R., & Hobbs, B. (2005). Governance regimes for large complex projects. *Project Management Journal, 36*(3), 42–50.

Morgan, D. L. (2007). Paradigms lost and pragmatism regained: Methodological implications of combining qualitative and quantitative methods. *Journal of Mixed Methods Research, 1*(1), 48–76.

Morris, P. W. G. (1994). *The management of projects: A new model.* London: Thomas Telford.

Morris, P. W. G., Crawford, L., Hodgson, D., Shepherd, M. M., & Thomas, J. (2006). Exploring the role of formal bodies of knowledge in defining a profession: The case of project management. *International Journal of Project Management, 24*(8), 710–721.

Mullen, E. J., & Noe, R. A. (1999). The mentoring information exchange: When do mentors seek information from their protégés? *Journal of Organizational Behavior, 20*(2), 233–242.

Müller, R. (2009). *Project governance.* Farnam, Surrey, UK: Gower.

Müller, R., & Turner, J. R. (2007). Matching the project manager's leadership style to project type. *International Journal of Project Management, 25*(1), 21–32.

Muriithi, N., & Crawford, L. (2003). Approaches to project management in Africa: Implications for international development projects. *International Journal of Project Management, 21*(5), 309–319.

Nogeste, K. (2006). Development of a method to improve the definition and alignment of intangible project outcomes with tangible project outputs. Unpublished doctoral dissertation, RMIT University—Melbourne.

Nogeste, K. (2010). Understanding mergers and acquisitions (M&As) from a program management perspective. *International Journal of Managing Projects in Business, 3*(1), 111–138.

Nogeste, K., & Walker, D. H. T. (2005). Project outcomes and outputs: Making the intangible tangible. *Measuring Business Excellence, 9*(4), 55–68.

Norrie, J. (2008). *Breaking through the project fog: How smart organizations achieve success by creating, selecting and executing on-strategy projects.* Toronto: John Wiley & Sons Canada Ltd.

Norrie, J., & Walker, D. H. T. (2004). A balanced scorecard approach to project management leadership. *Project Management Journal, 35*(4), 47–56.

Norrie, J. L. (2006). Improving results of project portfolio management in the public sector using a balanced scorecard approach. Unpublished doctoral dissertation, RMIT University—Melbourne.

OECD. (2007). *Sourcebook for evaluating global and regional partnership programs indicative principles and standards.* Washington, DC: Development Assistance Committee (DAC).

Office of Government Commerce. (2007). *Managing successful programmes.* London: The Stationary Office (TSO).

Olander, S., & Landin, A. (2005). Evaluation of stakeholder influence in the implementation of construction projects. *International Journal of Project Management, 23*(4), 321–328.

Oquist, P. (1978). The epistemology of action research. *Acta Sociologica, 21*(2), 143–163.

Overseas Development Administration. (1995). *Guidance note on how to do stakeholder analysis of aid projects and programmes.* London: Department for International Development.

Parker, S. K., Williams, H. M., & Turner, N. (2006). Modeling the antecedents of proactive behavior at work. *Journal of Applied Psychology, 91*(3), 636–652.

Pearsall, J., & Hanks, P. (Eds.). (2001). *The new Oxford dictionary of English.* Oxford, UK: Oxford University Press.

Pellegrinelli, S. (1997). Programme management: Organising project-based change. *International Journal of Project Management, 15*(3), 141–149.

Pettigrew, A., & Whittington, D. (2003). Complementarities in action: Organizational change and performance in BP and Unilever, 1985–2002. In A. M. Pettigrew, R. Whittington, L. Melin, C. Sánchez-Runde, F. A. J. van den Bosch, W. Ruigrok & T. Numagami (Eds.) *Innovative forms of organizing* (pp. 173–207). Thousand Oaks, CA: Sage.

Pinto, J. K., & Prescott, J. E. (1987). Variations in critical success factors over the stages in the project life cycle. *Journal of Management, 14*(1), 5–18.

Pinto, J. K., & Slevin, D. (1987). Critical factors in successful project implementation. *IEEE Transactions on Engineering Management, EM-34*(1), 22–27.

PMI (2004) *A guide to the project management body of knowledge.* (PMBOK® Guide) Sylva, NC: Author.

PMI (2005) *Post-disaster rebuild methodology.* Newtown Square, PA: Author.

PMI (2006a) *The standard for portfolio management.* Newtown Square, PA: Author.

PMI (2006b) *The standard for program management.* Newtown Square, PA: Author.

PMI (2008a) *A guide to the project management body of knowledge*—Fourth Edition, Newtown Square, PA: Author.

PMI (2008b) *The standard for program management.* Newtown Square, PA: Author.

Pollack, J. (2007). The changing paradigms of project management. *International Journal of Project Management, 25*(3), 266–274.

Popper, M., & Zakkai, E. (1994). Transactional, charismatic and transformational leadership: Conditions conducive to their predominance. *Leadership and Organisation Development Journal, 15*(6), 3–7.

Prilleltensky, I. (2001). Value-based praxis in community psychology: Moving toward social justice and social action. *American Journal of Community Psychology, 29*(5), 747.

Prilleltensky, I., & Totikidis, V. (2006). Engaging community in a cycle of praxis. *Community, Work and Family, 9*(1), 47–67.

Raelin, J. A. (2001). Public reflection as the basis of learning. *Management Learning, 32*(1), 11–30.

Raelin, J. A. (2007). Toward an epistemology of practice. *Academy of Management Learning & Education, 6*(4), 495–519.

Ramage, P., & Armstrong, A. (2005). Measuring success: Factors impacting on the implementation and use of performance measurement within Victoria's human services agencies. *Evaluation Journal of Australasia, 5*(2), 5–17.

Reeler, D. (2007). *A theory of social change and implications for practice, planning, monitoring and evaluation.* Community Development Resource Association (CDRA). Retrieved June 1, 2010, from www.cdra.org.za.

Remenyi, D., & Sherwood-Smith, M. (1998). Business benefits from information systems through an active benefits realization programme. *International Journal of Project Management, 16*(2), 81–98.

Remington, K., & Pollack, J. (2007). *Tools for complex projects.* Aldershot, UK: Gower.

Rickard, P. (Producer). (2000, June 10). Interview with Professor Susan Greenfield. *The Science Show* [Radio broadcast]. Sydney, Australia: Australian Broadcast Corporation. Retrieved June 1, 2010, from http://www.abc.net.au/rn/science/ss/stories/s137294.htm

Rose, J. (1997). Soft systems methodology as a social science research tool. *Systems Research and Behavioural Science, 14*(4), 249–258.

Roget, P. M., J. L. Roget, & S. R. Roget. 1980. *Roget's thesaurus of synonyms and antonyms.* New York: Modern Promotions.

Sankaran, S., Tay, B. H., & Orr, M. (2009). Managing organizational change by using soft systems thinking in action research projects. *International Journal of Managing Projects in Business, 2*(2), 179–197.

Schein, E. H. (1996). Three cultures of management: The key to organizational learning. *Sloan Management Review, 38*(1), 9–20.

Schön, D. A. (1983). *The reflective practitioner: How professionals think in action.* Aldershot, UK: BasiAshgate ARENA.

Senge, P., Kleiner, A., Roberts, C., Roth, G., & Smith, B. (1999). *The dance of change: The challenges of sustaining momentum in learning organisations.* New York: Doubleday.

Senge, P. M. (1990). *The fifth discipline: The art and practice of the learning organization.* Sydney, Australia: Random House.

Sense, A. J. (2005). *Cultivating situational learning within project management practice.* Unpublished doctoral dissertation, Macquarie University—Sydney.

Sense, A. J. (2007). *Cultivating learning within projects.* New York: Palgrave MacMillan.

Sewchurran, K. (2008). Toward an approach to create self-organising and reflexive information systems project practitioners. *International Journal of Managing Projects in Business, 1*(3), 316–333.

Shalin, D. N. (1992). Critical theory and the pragmatist challenge. *The American Journal of Sociology, 98*(2), 237–279.

Shamir, B., & Eilam, G. (2005). "What's your story?" A life-stories approach to authentic leadership development. *The Leadership Quarterly, 16*(3), 395–417.

Shenhar, A. J., Dvir, D., Levy, O., & Maltz, A. C. (2001). Project success: A multidimensional strategic concept. *Long Range Planning, 34*(6), 699–725.

Shenhar, A. L., & Dvir, D. (2004). How projects differ, and what to do about it. In P. W. G. Morris & J. K. Pinto (Eds.) *The Wiley guide to managing projects* (pp.1,265–1,286). New York: Wiley.

Sigsgaard, P. (2002). MSC approach: Monitoring without indicators. *Evaluation Journal of Australasia, 2*(1), 8–15.

Small, J. M. (2009). *The emergent realities of project praxis in socially complex project environments.* Unpublished doctoral dissertation, RMIT University—Melbourne.

Smith, C. (2007). *Making sense of project realities: Theory, practice and the pursuit of performance.* Aldershot, UK: Gower Publishing Ltd.

Smith, C., & Winter, M. (2010). The craft of project shaping. *International Journal of Managing Projects in Business, 3*(1), 46–60.

Smith, M. K. (2007) Action research. In *The encyclopedia of informal education.* Retrieved June 1, 2010, from www.infed.org/research/b-actres.htm

Smyth, H. (2008). The credibility gap in stakeholder management: ethics and evidence of relationship management. *Construction Management & Economics, 26*(6), 633–643.

Smyth, H. J., & Morris, P. W. G. (2007). An epistemological evaluation of research into projects and their management: Methodological issues. *International Journal of Project Management, 25*(4), 423–436.

Snowden, D. J., & Boone, M. E. (2007). A leader's framework for decision making. *Harvard Business Review, 85*(11), 69–76.

Söderlund, J. (2005). Developing project competence: Empirical regularities in competitive project operations. *International Journal of Innovation Management, 9*(4), 451–480.

Stame, N. (2004). Theory-based evaluation and types of complexity. *Evaluation, 10*(1), 58–76.

Steinfort, P. (2010). Understanding the antecedents of project management best practice: Lessons to be learned from aid relief projects. Unpublished doctoral dissertation, RMIT University—Melbourne.

Strauss, A., & Corbin, J. (1998). *Basics of qualitative research.* Thousand Oaks, CA: Sage Publications, Inc.

Szulanski, G. (1996). Exploring internal stickiness: Impediments to the transfer of best practice within the firm. *Strategic Management Journal, 17*, 27–43.

Thiry, M., & Deguire, M. (2007). Recent developments in project-based organisations. *International Journal of Project Management, 25*(7), 649–658.

Thite, M. (1999). Leadership styles in information technology projects. *International Journal of Project Management, 18*(2), 235–241.

Thomas, J., Delisle, C. L. & Jugdev, K. (2002). *Selling project management to senior executives: Framing the moves that matte.* Newtown Square, PA: Project Management Institute.

Thomas, J., & Mullaly, M. (2008). *Researching the value of project management.* Newtown Square, PA: Project Management Institute.

Toor, S. R., & Ofori, G. (2007). Leadership for future construction industry agenda for authentic leadership. *International Journal of Project Management, 26*(6), 620–630.

Trompenaars, F. (1993). *Riding the waves of culture: Understanding cultural diversity in business.* London: Economics Books.

Trompenaars, F., & Hampden-Turner, C. (2004). *Managing people: Across cultures.* Chichester, England: Capstone.

Trompenaars, F., & Prud'homme, P. (2004). *Managing change across corporate cultures.* London: Piatkus.

Turner, J. R., & Cochrane, R. A. (1993). The goals and methods matrix: Coping with projects with ill-defined goals and/or methods of achieving them. *International Journal of Project Management, 11*(2), 93–102.

Turner, J. R., & Keegan, A. (2001). Mechanisms of governance in the project-based organization: Roles of the broker and steward. *European Management Journal, 19*(3), 254–267.

Turner, J. R., & Müller, R. (2005). The project manager's leadership style as a success factor on projects: A literature review. *Project Management Journal, 36*(2), 49–61.

Turner, J. R., Muller, R., & Dulewicz, V. (2009). Comparing the leadership styles of functional and project managers. *International Journal of Managing Projects in Business, 2*(2), 198–216.

Turner, J. R., & Simister, S. J. (2000). *Gower handbook of project management.* Aldershot, England and Burlington, VT: Gower.

UNICEF (1990). *A UNICEF guide for monitoring and evaluation: Making a difference?* New York: Author.

United Nations Development Programme (UNDP). (2002). *Handbook on monitoring and evaluating for results.* New York: Author, Evaluation Office.

United Nations Development Programme (UNDP). (2003). *United Nations Development Programme millennium development goals.* New York: Oxford University Press.

USAID (1973). *The logical framework: Modifications based on experience.* Washington, DC: USAID—Program Methods & Evaluation Division.

Walker, D. H. T., Bourne, L., & Rowlinson, S. (2008). Stakeholders and the supply chain. In D. H. T. Walker & S. Rowlinson (Eds.) *Procurement systems: A cross industry project management perspective* (pp. 70–100). Abingdon, Oxon: Taylor & Francis.

Walker, D. H. T., Cicmil, S., Thomas, J., Anbari, F. T., & Bredillet, C. (2008). Collaborative academic/practitioner research in project management: Theory and models. *International Journal of Managing Projects in Business, 1*(1), 17–32.

Walker, D. H. T., & Nogeste, K. (2008). Performance measures and project procurement. In D. H. T. Walker & S. Rowlinson (Eds.) *Procurement systems: A cross industry project management perspective* (pp. 177–210). Abingdon, Oxon: Taylor & Francis.

Walker, D. H. T., Segon, M., & Rowlinson, S. (2008). Business ethics and corporate citizenship. In D. H. T. Walker & S. Rowlinson (Eds.) *Procurement systems: A cross industry project management perspective* (pp. 101–139). Abingdon, Oxon: Taylor & Francis.

Wang, E., Chou, H. W., & Jiang, J. (2005). The impacts of charismatic leadership style on team cohesiveness and overall performance during ERP implementation. *International Journal of Project Management, 23*(3), 173–180.

Wang, X. (2002). Developing a true sense of professional community: An important matter for PM professionalism. *Project Management Journal, 33*(1), 5.

Weick, K. E. (1988). Enacted sense-making in crisis situation. *Journal of Management Studies, 25*(4), 305–317.

Weick, K. E. (1989). Theory construction as disciplined imagination. *Academy of Management Review, 14*(4), 516–531.

Weick, K. E. (1995a). *Sense-making in organizations.* Thousand Oaks, CA: Sage.

Weick, K. E. (1995b). What theory is not, theorizing is. *Administrative Science Quarterly, 40*(3), 385–390.

Weick, K. E. (1999). Theory construction as disciplined reflexivity: Tradeoffs in the 90s. *Academy of Management Review, 24*(4), 797–806.

Weick, K. E. (2001a). Leadership as the legitimation of doubt. In W. Bennis, G. M. Spreitzer, & T. G. Cummings, *The future of leadership: Today's top leadership thinkers speak to tomorrow's leaders* (pp. 91–102). San Francisco: Jossey-Bass.

Weick, K. E. (2001b). *Making sense of the organization.* Oxford: Blackwell Publishers.

Weick, K. E., Sutcliffe, K. M., & Obstfeld, D. (2005). Organizing and the process of sense-making. *Organization Science, 16*(4), 409–421.

Wenger, E. C., McDermott, R., & Snyder, W. M. (2002). *Cultivating communities of practice.* Boston: Harvard Business School Press.

Whittington, R., & Pettigrew, A. (2003). Complementarities thinking. In A. M. Pettigrew, R. Whittington, L. Melin, C. Sánchez-Runde, F. A. J. van den Bosch, W. Ruigrok & T. Numagami (Eds.), *Innovative forms of organizing* (pp. 125–132). Thousand Oaks, CA: Sage.

Whittington, R., Pettigrew, A., Peck, S., Fenton, E., & Conyon, M. (1999). Change and complementarities in the new competitive landscape: A European panel study, 1992–1996. *Organization Science, 10*(5), 583.

Whitty, S. J., & Schulz, M. F. (2007). The impact of Puritan ideology on aspects of project management. *International Journal of Project Management, 25*(1), 10–20.

Williams, T. (2007). *Post-project reviews to gain effective lessons learned.* Newtown Square, PA: Project Management Institute.

Williams, T., Eden, C., Ackermann, F., & Tait, A. (1995). Vicious circles of parallelism. *International Journal of Project Management, 13*(3), 151–155.

Williams, T., Klakegg, O. J., Magnussen, O. M., & Glasspool, H. (2010). An investigation of governance frameworks for public projects in Norway and the UK. *International Journal of Project Management, 28*(1), 40–50.

Williams, T. M. (1999). The need for new paradigms for complex projects. *International Journal of Project Management, 17*(5), 269–273.

Williams, T. M., Samset, K., & Sunnevåg, K. J. (Eds.). (2009). *Making essential choices with scant information: Front-end decision making in major projects.* Basingstoke, UK: Palgrave Macmillan.

Winch, G. M. (2001). Governing the project process: A conceptual framework. *Construction Management and Economics, 19*(8), 799–808.

Winch, G. M. (2004). Managing project stakeholders. In P. W. G. Morris & J. K. Pinto (Eds.), *The Wiley guide to managing projects* (pp. 321–339). New York: Wiley.

Winter, M. (2009). Using soft systems methodology to structure project definition. In T. M. Williams, K. Samset, & K. J. Sunnevåg (Eds.), *Making essential choices with scant information: Front-end decision making in major projects* (pp. 125–144). Basingstoke, UK: Palgave Macmillan.

Winter, M., Andersen, E. S., Elvin, R., & Levene, R. (2006). Focusing on business projects as an area for future research: An exploratory discussion of four different perspectives. *International Journal of Project Management, 24*(8), 699–709.

Winter, M., & Checkland, P. (2003). Soft systems: A fresh perspective for project management. *Proceedings of the Institution of Civil Engineers: Civil Engineering, 156*(4), 187–192.

Winter, M., & Smith, C. (2006). *EPSRC Network 2004–2006 rethinking project management final report* (Rep. No. 15). Manchester: EPSRC.

Winter, M., Smith, C., Morris, P. W. G., & Cicmil, S. (2006). Directions for future research in project management: The main findings of a UK government-funded research network. *International Journal of Project Management, 24*(8), 638–649.

The World Bank. (2004). Local pathways to global development, marking five years of the World Bank indigenous knowledge for development program (Rep. No. 282). Knowledge and Learning Group—Africa Region: Author.

York, J. (2009). Pragmatic sustainability: Translating environmental ethics into competitive advantage. *Journal of Business Ethics, 85*(0), 97–109.

Zuber-Skerritt, O. (2002). A model for designing action learning and action research programs. *The Learning Organization, 9*(4), 143–149.

Zuber-Skeritt, O., & Perry, C. (2002). Action research within organisations and university thesis writing. *The Learning Organization, 9*(4), 171–179.

Zwikael, O. (2008). Top management involvement in project management: Exclusive support practices for different project scenarios. *International Journal of Managing Projects in Business, 1*(3), 387–403.

Appendix–Abbreviations

Ⓐ	action in an action learning cycle
ABS	assembly breakdown structure
AIPM	Australian Institute of Project Management
AR	action research
AUD	Australian dollars
AusAID	Australian Department of Aid–Australia's Commonwealth Government aid agency
BOK	body of knowledge
CATWOE	mnemonic of Client, Actors, Transformation, Worldview, Owner,Environment
CEO	chief executive officer
CIDA	Canadian International Development Agency
COO	chief operations officer
CoP	community of practice
CSC	critical success criteria
CSF	critical success factors
DAC	Development Assistance Committee
Danida	Danish International Development Agency
DFID	Department for International Development
EQ	emotional intelligence quotient
GLOBE	Global Leadership and Organizational Effectiveness
IQ	intelligence quotient
IS	information systems
IT	information technology
LogFrame	the logical framework approach
LFA	the logical framework approach

M&E	monitoring and evaluation
MCG	Melbourne Cricket Ground
MQ	management intelligence quotient
M_R	research methodology
M_{PC}	method for problem-solving
NGO	non government organization
NCTP	novelty, complexity, technology, and pace
OBS	objectives breakdown structure
OECD	Organization for Economic Co-operation and Development
OGC	Office of Government Commerce (in the UK)
PBS	product breakdown structure
PDRM	Post Disaster Rebuild Methodology
PhD	Doctor of Philosophy
PM	project management
PMI	Project Management Institute
PMBOK	project management body of knowledge
PMBOK® Guide	A Guide to the Project Management Body of Knowledge
PQR	What to do (P), How to do it (Q), and Why to do it (R)
PRINCE2	PRojects IN Controlled Environments, version 2
PSA	Paul Steinfort and Associates
QA	quality assurance
®	reflection activity in an action learning cycle
RMIT	Royal Melbourne Institute of Technology University
ROI	return on investment
SIG	special interest group
SSM	soft systems methodology
TQM	total quality management
UK	United Kingdom
UN	United Nations
UNDP	United Nations Development Programme
USAID	United States Agency for International Development
VBRRA	Victorian Bushfire Reconstruction and Recovery Authority
WBS	work breakdown structure

Author Bios

Paul Steinfort has extensive Project Planning and Management experience and knowledge in the Project Management in both the built and rebuilding environment at the working, management and executive level. He can bring to any project an approach deep in project management knowledge, but with a clear and practical understanding. He has experience, over many years, in an extraordinary range & number of projects and places and retains a strong interest in the practices & skills needed to support that into successful outcomes.

He has served as CEO of PSA Project Management for over 20 years and has led the way in new Project Management implementation for major projects such as the MCG Re-development, and for Post Tsunami, Earthquake, Bushfire and Cyclone Programmes in Australia and Asia (Aceh, Indonesia, India, Asia, Darwin, Victoria, Australia.

He has approximately 40 years experience in a very wide range of projects and environments and combines this with proven theory and applications necessary for the successful mentoring or implementation of project management in post disaster or "at risk" environments and master training and mentoring of those involved, at all levels.

He has lectured at Graduate and Post Graduate level in Project and Programme Management and maintains both practical and academic involvement in a wide range of project, community, not for profit, aid and programme recovery activities.

Dr. Derek Walker is Professor of Project Management and Director of Research at the School of Property, Construction and Project Management, RMIT University. He worked in various project management roles in the UK, Canada, and Australia for 16 years before commencing his academic career in 1986. He obtained a Master of Science from the University of Aston (Birmingham) in 1978, and a PhD in 1995 from RMIT University (Melbourne). He has written over 200 peer reviewed papers and book chapters. His most recent books include Klakegg, O. J., Williams, T., Walker, D. H. T., Andersen, B. and Magnussen, O. M. (2010) *Early Warning Signs in Complex Projects*, Newtown Square, PA, USA, Project Management Institute and Walker, D. H. T. and Rowlinson, S., Eds. (2008). *Procurement Systems—A Cross Industry Project Management Perspective.* Series Procurement Systems—A Cross Industry Project Management Perspective. Abingdon, Oxon, Taylor & Francis.

His research interests centre on innovation diffusion of information and communication technologies, knowledge management, project management and project procurement systems.

He is director of the Doctor of Project Management (DPM) academic program at RMIT University http://dhtw.tce.rmit.edu.au/pmgt/ and also teaches into the Master of Project Management (MPM) academic program at RMIT. He is editor of The *International Journal of Managing Projects in Business* for Emerald Insight http://info.emeraldinsight.com/products/journals/journals.htm?PHPSESSID=j0b m25095pn370h1fvdobdsti4&id=ijmpb and is a member of the editorial board of the Project Management Journal, The Learning Organization, Construction Innovation and several other journals.